NARRATIVES OF THE CHINESE ECONOMIC REFORMS

NARRATIVES OF THE CHINESE ECONOMIC REFORMS

Individual Pathways from Plan to Market

Edited by
Dorothy J. Solinger

The Edwin Mellen Press
Lewiston•Queenston•Lampeter

Library of Congress Cataloging-in-Publication Data

Narratives of the Chinese economic reforms : individual pathways from plan to market / edited by Dorothy J. Solinger.

p. cm.

Includes bibliographical references (p.).

ISBN 0-7734-5929-4

I. Title.

hors série.

A CIP catalog record for this book is available from the British Library.

The Edwin Mellen Press
Box 450
Lewiston, New York
USA 14092-0450

The Edwin Mellen Press
Box 67
Queenston, Ontario
CANADA L0S 1L0

The Edwin Mellen Press, Ltd.
Lampeter, Ceredigion, Wales
UNITED KINGDOM SA48 8LT

Printed in the United States of America

We dedicate this book to the vivid and sympathetic individuals who spoke with us about their lives, and hope we did them justice.

Dorothy J. Solinger also dedicates the book to Marcia Pastor Weiland, who was thrilled by the tale of Zheng Erji and who, in the last years of her life, was so kind as often to encourage the writing of Zheng's story.

Table of Contents

Preface

It is perhaps quite fitting that the narratives brought together in this volume focus on the stories of individuals. After all, one of the premises of China's economic reforms is that the unleashing of market forces will produce a new type of subject, a risk-bearing individual "responsible for his/her own profits and losses" whose productive energies can be developed through the pursuit of economic self-interest in a free market. However, the narratives presented here tell rather a different story: China's economic reforms of the last quarter century are revealed to be a much more contingent process in which the twists and turns of policy have afforded unparalleled opportunities for wealth accumulation for a few, while dispossessing a vast majority of others. These stories repeatedly demonstrate the importance of social connections, timing, and prior formations of political and cultural capital as critical factors in determining one's success or failure. Yet one's inability to prosper is attributed to a failure to adapt to the harsh new "realities" of market socialism. The individual is incited to a process of "self-development," in which a prior self can be made "liquid" (Baumann 2000) in a process of perpetual self-transformation.

To be liquid, one must not be so tied to one's formation as a subject that one fails to recognize when one is presented with opportunities to reinvent oneself, whether this takes the form of job retraining or taking up the challenge of the market through the exercise of entrepreneurial initiative (as evidenced by Lei Guang's migrant entrepreneur). What the narratives collected here clearly demonstrate is that success in the new economy is very much tied to the ability of actors to convert prior forms of cultural and political capital into money capital. Hence the determination of success or failure is anything but a level playing field but is contingent on one's access to convertible forms of capital.

The newsworthiness of China's transformation appears, therefore, to be a highly schizophrenic one. Either it is an unparalleled success story about the power of the market to create wealth and generate economic growth, or it is a tragic narrative of dispossession, growing social inequality, and environmental degradation. The paradox is that both of these possibilities appear to be true at the same time (an irony well captured by Sturgeon). Moreover, the social contradictions produced by the reforms are fully acknowledged by China's leadership, especially as concerns about social "disorder" and localized popular resistance have triggered alarms about the sustainability of the economic reforms (as noted by Rocca). Indeed, some have suggested that in this renewed concern for poverty alleviation, China is formulating an alternative model to the hegemonic model of the Washington Consensus. However, if the Beijing Consensus argues for economic development with a human face, it is no less based on the hegemony of the market as the primary agency for development (cf. Ramo 2004). The premise that "development is the necessary logic" (*fazhan shi ying daoli*) in the project of government has allowed market principles to overrule more overtly social concerns. The threat of "chaos" (*luan*) is what mobilizes policies of poverty alleviation in which the dynamism of the market must be brought into balance with the social contradictions it engenders. Poverty alleviation, therefore, is articulated as a project of crisis management, but many of the narratives in this volume show how projects of local development exacerbate increasing inequalities rather than resolving them by providing new spaces of opportunity for a few (as demonstrated by Oakes and Sturgeon).

In her critique of the mythos of how to become a successful person, Hairong Yan cites the metaphor of stir-frying as a way of speaking about the convertibility of value in Hua Min's refusal to be turned into an exemplar. Stir-frying is also something that you can do with stock shares (*chao gufen*), a constant churning of your portfolio to maximize returns, an activity that has become something of a past-time for millions of retired Chinese urbanites who dabble in penny stocks as a leisured game of risk that takes its thrills in profits and losses. However, one could say that the whole society is, in a sense, being stir-fried, in which the constant churning of what was once was the stable foundation upon which one could build a future is being dismantled in the process of converting assets into entrepreneurial capital in the hands of a few (a process poignantly captured by Kernen). Only if the rapid pace of change can be sustained, then the forces of social instability produced by these very changes will somehow be resolved through the dynamism of the market itself. This premise seems to be an enormous leap of faith in the power of the market to regulate itself, a gamble that is no less grand than the hubris of the Great Leap Forward (Mao's 1957 policy that staked all on a poorly planned mass mobilization of labor away from agriculture to large-scale construction projects that resulted in widespread famine). Many of the narratives in this volume (in particular, Kernen, Rocca, Solinger, and Yan) document the human costs of this stir-frying, the pressures that it puts on individuals, and how the structure of the family must serve as a shock absorber for the pressures resulting from the restructuring of the workplace.

How, then, does one measure the aggregate success or failure of such an economic calculus? In so doing, what costs are not accounted for? This seems to be the question that Yan asks when she speaks of the subterranean experiences of the migrant worker as a parallel mode of accumulation, in which the pain of labor and the stresses of social deprivation ceaselessly mount up as a call for social responsibility. What political form can this plea for social responsibility take? How can it be articulated in a fashion that will not be dismissed as hopelessly out-of-joint with the times? And what should be the role of the concerned scholar who chronicles the mounting up of this debt against the grain of the new "common sense?" Perhaps, when one records one's informants dredging up the Mao era as a form of social critique, we might refrain from labeling such moments as mere nostalgic longing for a past that is irrevocably lost and gone but see them instead as articulations of an alternate reality, the imagining of a hypothetical "what if" that can cut through the reigning market logics of the present to suggest other kinds of political possibility.[1] Neoliberal logics are premised on a radical negation of past social formations so that the ground can be cleared for the pure instantiation of the self-regulating truth of the market (Lemke 2001). For the scholar, a failure to challenge this overturning of value is to be complicit with this erasure. The stories told in this volume, therefore, provide a thoughtful balancing of the record.

Ann Anagnost
August 21, 2005

---

[1] This notion of "alternate reality" as a formulation that could displace "nostalgia" as a frame for understanding these evocations of the socialist past was co-developed in a conversation with David Davies as we wandered through one of the new old towns being developed in and around Shanghai in August 2005.

References:

Baumann, Zygmont
2000 Liquid Modernity. Cambridge: Polity Press.

Lemke, Thomas
2001 "The Birth of Bio-Politics": Michel Foucault's Lecture at the Collège de France on Neo-Liberal Governmentality. *Economy and Society* 30(2):190-207.

Ramo, Joshua Cooper
2004 The Beijing Consensus. London: Foreign Policy Centre (available online).

Acknowledgments

This book's existence is owed to the urgings of several people and also to one institution. First, the institution: the Center for Asian Studies at the University of California, Irvine, generously provided the funding for the initial meeting, in May 2004, of the group of scholars who became the authors of this book (and later, for the preparation of the publication). Next, there is my late aunt, Marcia Weiland, who loved the story of Zheng Erji, and had been begging me to write it up for a number of years before she insisted that I recite it to her one last time on her death-bed in October 2003.

After the meeting ended, Thomas P. Bernstein, who had attended the entire workshop, encouraged the publication of the papers, judging that they could be very useful in the classroom. But the project languished for some months, until Russell Dalton, then Director of the Center for the Study of Democracy at UCI, persuaded the editor that funded meetings at universities should not just disappear, but deserve to appear later in print. Even still, perhaps nothing further would have happened had Katherine Carlitz, also having expressed enthusiasm for the idea behind the set of papers, not told the editor about The Edwin Mellen Press. We all are very grateful for the support and good suggestions of these friends.

Introduction

Much scholarship has targeted China's monumental movement from a plan-regulated, socialist economy to one primarily driven by market forces, and the attendant social metamorphoses that were the offshoots of that shift. By this point, two and a half decades into this ongoing transformation, most treatises, however, have a macro focus, having been pitched either at a collective or a societal-wide level. The majority of them, as well, are written either from a political or a sociological perspective. We know of no specific volume that aims its gaze directly and solely upon particular, ordinary individuals. To tell the stories of a set of such people is our purpose in this study.

The project published here began with a one-day workshop at the University of California, Irvine in May 2004, under the sponsorship of its Center for Asian Studies. Five of the authors whose work is presented here—Lei Guang, Yan Hairong, Tim Oakes, Dorothy Solinger, and Janet Sturgeon—delivered papers at that meeting, along with Mei Zhan of the University's Anthropology Department. The objective was for each of us to delineate one remarkable person we had gotten to know in the course of our own fieldwork. That person was to be one whose life experiences over the past couple of decades represented a compelling case of negotiation with what was, for that individual, the initially unfamiliar forces of the market, and/or with the changing face of the state in the wake of the market's rebirth in China. Later, papers were solicited from Antoine Kernen and Jean-Louis Rocca, in order to diversify our set of characters.

While Kernen and Rocca were able to supply the sagas of once-state-sectoral workers now dismissed from their jobs—one a male from the northeast, the other a woman from Beijing--all the rest were peasants, at least for most of their lives. These other figures are a male minority-group member from southwestern Yunnan province, whose job was administrative village head, but who refashioned himself into a mining contractor, emerging as an overall winner in the reform period; a female farmer, domestic worker, and saleswoman from the eastern province of Jiangsu, who may be seen as successful by others but who experiences much ambivalence and even angst about her own achievements; a male from the southwest Guizhou countryside who has been a farmer, a village chief and itinerant trader, overall, another winner; a male migrant who dropped out of high school and became a construction worker and later a contractor, after departing from the central Chinese province of Anhui and settling in Beijing; and a peasant woman from a village outside the central Chinese city of Wuhan, who married an urban man after coming to the city to work in a shoe factory, later acquiring an urban household registration, but still suffering continuously, as she bumped up repeatedly against state regulations and regulators.

Our narratives envision these people sometimes as victims, other times as hustlers and victors. Their personal encounters with the changed state in the course of economic "reform" have frustrated yet enabled them. They are people whose strivings have been both licit and illicit, as they reached out for recognition, riches, or simple sustenance. Most of these individuals have remade themselves and their own identities once or even several times over recent years, in the process skirting governmental rules while occasionally even prodding system change within their own small corners of the country.

We have here a mixture of gender, locale, ethnicity and occupation. Each person we describe is a vibrant individual, one whose choices and actions exhibit guts and energy, grit and nerve, initiative and determination. Each of the tales demonstrates both the increased possibilities as well as the ongoing constraints these individuals encountered—and then navigated—as they set out to forge changed selves and to experiment and, so they hoped, to benefit from the reduced restrictions offered by the post-1978 Chinese political economy. We admire their pluck and celebrate the successes of our subjects, even as we empathize with their trials. Though in most cases we have altered their names in the telling, we dedicate this volume to their savvy, their triumphs, and their travails.

Refusing Success, Refusing "Voice": the Other Story of Accumulation

Hairong Yan

Much of the legitimacy of the post-Mao reform is created and reinforced by representations of successful individuals whose talent, personal quality, and efforts seem to be rightfully rewarded by the market economy. The market economy offers opportunities for success for the educated elites, as well as for shrewd semi-literate peasants. The market economy may not be a wholly fair playing field and the world should not forget those unfortunate migrant women toiling in sweatshop conditions...nevertheless, opportunity is a mischievous star glittering in the air for everyone to grab, including those migrant women. Or so it goes. This story sells on both shores of the Pacific, albeit in different ways. Lo, the media in China offers testimonies of a handful who have succeeded against the odds and of many more who vow to follow suit and struggle for success. The destiny of China seems to be cast in the long-tested dialectical line: the future is bright and the path is bumpy. And the media in the United States tries to balance between an excitement for the rapidly opening market in China and an obligation to lament the human rights violations in sweatshop conditions, in other words, between the interests of transnational capital and the interests of liberal human rights groups and US-based unions, and between the capital logic of engaging the new China market and the old political logic of anti-communism. Although the balance tips more to one side or the other now and then, exposés about China betray a familiar pattern.

Beneath these hegemonic frameworks that organize our perceptions of the reality, migrant workers accumulate their subterranean experiences—experiences that cannot be subsumed by these frameworks. They accumulate these unceasing experiences, which are not only their own, but also those of their relatives, friends, and acquaintances. From time to time these experiences may be such an overwhelming and crushing burden that they have to forget in order to live; from time to time these experiences are scattered between the countryside and the city and are hard to piece together. It may be difficult to say what the accumulation will amount to and what kind of quantitative-to-qualitative transformation will give it meaning. But as the reform goes on, the subterranean experiences keep accumulating, in a spectral relationship with the accumulation of Gross Domestic Product.

A Successful Migrant Who Refuses to Talk

Hua Min seems to be a successful migrant by the usual criteria. She left her home village in Sichuan for Beijing in 1982. For the first eight years of her migrancy, Hua Min worked as a domestic in Beijing, during which time she studied part-time for a tertiary diploma. Without seeing much of a future for herself in Beijing, she went south to Shenzhen in 1992 and found a job as a saleswoman in a telephone company. Her sales record was good enough that she was able to persuade her company to move her household registration from her home village to Shenzhen. In 1997 she moved back to Beijing to be united with her husband who is a Beijing resident. By the time we met in 1999, Hua Min was an independent retailer, had an urban household registration, a husband, who is a state employee, and a young daughter. Not only could her case easily be seen as an individual success story of class mobility, but it could also easily be cited as "evidence" for the logic of self-development in the market economy—if one intends to develop oneself and is willing to eat all the necessary bitterness in the process, then one can succeed. The logic of self-development is a micrology of the discourse of development, or the latter is self-development writ large.

The discourses of development and self-development, championed by post-Mao market reform, are supposed to have rendered class (*jieji*) an invalid analytical category for contemporary Chinese society. A recent publication authored by scholars at Chinese Academy of Social Sciences used *jieceng* (strata) as an analytical category for social classification.[1] *Jieceng* stresses mobility and fluidity. Individual instances of social mobility are also particularly understood as examples that each contain the truth of self-development. Millions of such stories are promoted by the media and, despite a myriad of vicissitudes, tell of a coherent development of the self. I had heard about Hua Min through other migrants and I was curious what she thought of her own experiences, as she seemed to have all the necessary ingredients for such a story.

Hua Min, however, had subtly tried to avoid talking to me, which I only learned after we became quite familiar. At that time I was slow in following her cues and just kept trying. We did not get a chance for an extended conversation until I waited to meet her for almost an hour in a context of an accidental mix-up. In that first conversation I asked her whether she interpreted her story as a "success" story. Hua Min thought for a while and replied:

> There are many contingent elements in my success. This success is not a necessary (*biran*) one. It's not that once you make all your efforts, you will get it. Moreover, I don't think all the hardships I have experienced can be balanced off by these things [what are considered to be her success]. For example, having a diploma doesn't mean that you can find a job—there are too many with diplomas who cannot find jobs. The reason why I could stay in Beijing is because of my husband, but this affair itself was very fortuitous (*ouran*).

> I came to Beijing seventeen years ago in 1982 and moved to Shenzhen in 1992. It happened to be the year of Deng Xiaoping's Southern Tour (*nanxun*) and the "bubble economy" was at its hottest. I happened to have the problem of my household registration resolved just before the economy slid down hill. After the Asian Financial Crisis, migrants were having a hard time. It was a coincidence that my household registration was resolved before this bad time. From 1978 to 1983 about twenty thousand women came from my county to Beijing. Later village and township enterprises at home attracted most of them back. These years, these enterprises are declining and most of the women have come back out again. Of the twenty thousand, only two of us managed to stay on in Beijing, both because of our Beijing husbands. Two out of twenty thousand. It's extremely fortuitous.

Hua Min is aware that the media enthusiastically recruits migrant success stories. She could use her story to "stir fry" (*chao*) herself, to package herself as "a beautiful bubble" or a model of success to show others and thus to increase her social recognition and value. She has avoided reporters who are eager for such stories. The star migrant in Shenzhen, Anzi, who made her name by "stir frying" her stories, has built a migrant workers' club in Shezhen. The foundation slogan of Anzi's migrant club is that "everyone can become the sun" (*renren dou keyi chengwei taiyang*). Hua Min shook her head over this slogan. She herself once submitted an essay about the experiences of her first year in Beijing to the "*dagong* (itinerant urban worker) *Beijing*" column of *Beijing Youth Journal* (*Beijing qingnianbao*). The essay was not accepted for publication. However, the editor told her that if she would write on the topic of "I married a Beijinger," it would be printed the next day. Hua Min refused. She is unwilling to do so because she has a very different understanding of migrant experiences.

Hua Min and Her Siblings: Subterranean Experiences

Hua Min's refusal of her voice and her insistence that the mainstream representation of her "success" cannot do justice to her experiences pushed me to understand her story as belonging to subterranean experiences. These are experiences of migrant workers that are generated immanently by the grand market system, minutely, hourly, daily, on and on, unceasingly. They are subterranean because these migrants' life, labor, aspirations, and desire are becoming part of the grand market system, but cannot be justly accounted for by the mainstream discourse of development. The unceasing subterranean experiences accumulate, but this accumulation does not follow the logic of accumulation of *suzhi* (quality) that promises self-development and self-fulfillment in the market economy, as we will see shortly. *Suzhi* is a prominent keyword in post-Mao China and is used to index a range of characteristics considered essential for building a developed market-oriented economy and society. The improvement of the quality of the people and of each individual is deemed to be a necessary condition for national and individual development.[2]

Hua Min, the eldest of three daughters, left her home village in Sichuan in 1982, after finishing high school. Her desire to leave the countryside was shaped by her mother, who was recruited to work in the city as a factory worker in the 1950s, as a young woman, and who returned to the countryside several years later. The return of the mother's status to rural was a major disappointment for the mother herself. Her stint in the city seemed to have left her deeply alienated from rural life, rural labor, and even from her family members. "Mother has envied the city life since then and thinks the rural life is beneath her. Even as a child I felt that my mother was wronged, that she shouldn't have belonged to the countryside, and shouldn't ever have belonged to our humble family." Hua Min learned to view rural life through the mother's eyes: the countryside is to be escaped from.

When Hua Min was in high school in 1980-82, stories of others going to the city as migrants were already being circulated. Indeed, some villagers in the commune near the county seat were already migrating. After finishing high school and failing the national entrance exam, Hua Min began to participate in rural labor. Land was distributed to sub-team groups, but the commune was not yet dissolved, as it soon would be. Thus labor was still collective, evaluated daily in terms of work points. After the land collectivization in the late 1950s, rural society was organized into a three-tiered structure: productive teams, brigades, and communes, with the production team being the basic production and accounting unit. Hua Min caught the tail end of this collective era. However, already in 1977, the national entrance examination system was reinstituted, shortly after Mao's passing in 1976. This score-based, strictly implemented meritocratic process selects a minority of high school graduates for tertiary education. Criticized and abolished in the Cultural Revolution (1966-1976), the system after 1977 took the place of the Cultural Revolution practice that sorted out candidates for college education from the ranks of workers, peasants, and soldiers (so-called "*gong-nong-bing xue yuan*") on the basis of a range of factors, including the "political soundness" of the individual and local recommendations. After 1977 the restored examination system became the main venue through which rural high school students competed among themselves and with urban students for opportunities for higher education and urban state-salaried employment. A rural high school education did not culturally or technically prepare a rural student for rural labor, even though it is likely that one who passed through it would fail in the national exam for college and end up having to work in the fields. Her high school experience in fact had oriented Hua Min toward an urban-based modernity and alienated her from her co-villagers and rural labor.

> Villagers cared about whether you could do well in the field and didn't care whether you went to high school or not. If you're capable, they would award you with higher work points. Then I also disliked rural chores (*nonghuo*). So I avoided talking to people and pouted my lips all day long.

The full work points for a day were ten. Hua Min recalled that her sister—who did not go to high school—could earn five, while she herself could earn only three.

> Perhaps I didn't have the strength or maybe I just wasn't experienced. If you always lag behind, then others wouldn't think much of you. My younger sister was taller and stronger. She didn't go to high school, but she's good at farm work. All seemed easy for her. I couldn't catch up with

> her. After my graduation, I wanted to become a bookkeeper. Those days a bookkeeper in the village was already an intellectual. But nobody elected me, because I wasn't good at farm work and seemed incapable. People elected a person with junior high education.

Tempted by the beginning of the trend of migration, Hua Min managed to go to Beijing at the end of 1982 through a connection she located—her neighbor had a cousin working in Beijing as a *baomu* (domestic). So she worked as a *baomu* for the next eight years.

Hua Min's experience of alienation and departure from rural life is quite representative of many in her generation of migrants. She identified strongly with the main character, Gao Jialin in the 1980s novel "Ren Sheng." Gao Jialin, also a high school graduate who failed the national entrance exam, was devastated after returning to his rural home. When he subsequently lost his teaching position in the village school, the author sighed for him, "*Nongmin* (peasant or farmer)! He knew all their hardships and greatness! Although he never looked down upon any *nongmin*, he had never prepared himself to be one!"[3] The story was about this young intellectual's intimate yet alienated relationship with late-Mao and post-Mao rurality and his efforts to locate his social position and agency. Hua Min cried when she read the novel. Other 1980s high school graduates-turned-migrants with whom I have become acquainted also saw themselves in Gao Jialin. Hua Min is a little different from most other migrants of her generation in that she experienced this alienation both through her mother as well as on her own.

However, much as Hua Min was very determined to leave the countryside, in her subsequent years of being a migrant worker, she developed a strong sense of migrant rurality. For Hua Min, this rurality is built on her familiar experiences of rural life, but is not based on a nostalgia for or romanticism over the countryside, nor is it place-based. In fact, Hua Min has more critical observations than many migrants about the limitations of the rural community. Her sense of rurality is a migrant rurality, reflected in her bitter observation that "there is no future for us in the city, but there is no place for us to return to in the countryside." She acquired this perception through a series of hardships mixed with hope, disappointment, and radical disorientation.

By 1988, six years after her arrival in Beijing, Hua Min had worked for a number of families as a domestic. She began to worry about her future. At the time a "fever" to learn English was spreading in the city and a number of schools came into existence, promising to provide an education and grant a diploma. Hua Min thought if she earned a diploma in Beijing, she could be an English teacher in her home village. She was willing to go back to be a teacher, because that seemed better than being a *baomu* in the city. "It's honorable to be a teacher. You know there is no future for a domestic in the city." With this plan in mind, Hua Min spent the next three years working part time and going to classes. She borrowed money to pay the tuition and, whenever she could, she worked as a part-time domestic in exchange for free room and/or board. Sometimes when she could not find a place to stay, she would sneak into the classroom at night and sleep on the desks. During these three years Hua Min always had sleep deficit, skipped meals from time to time, and was often half starved. With little cash income, she even had to ask for money from her parents sometimes, instead of remitting money home. In order to support Hua Min's education and while also subsidizing her parents, Hua Min's youngest sister Hua Jie went to Shenzhen to find work.

Of all the women from her county working as domestics in Beijing, nobody else tried to go to school. Her migrant friends often praised her, but they doubted what she could do with this education. Hua Min herself was sometimes doubtful too, suspecting that she was deluding herself. At the end of the three years, she was basically penniless and in debt. And she did not even get a diploma, because the school had only been informally set up by a few professors of one university and was not formally attached to or even acknowledged by that university. Nevertheless, Hua Min returned home to try to begin a teaching career. Her father had had enough of bitterness working as a substitute teacher: a substitute teacher is worked to exhaustion and takes the rap, but derives no benefits. Even though Hua Min was willing to take such a job, she could not find one. She thought about finding a teaching position in a poorer mountainous area, but she had no contacts whatsoever.

By then it was 1991. Hua Min was lost about what she could do in the countryside, while feeling the heavy burden of sacrifice that her parents and sister had made for her education. Her parents urged her to go out again. "Actually my parents didn't quite know about the situation for me in the city. They tended to think that it should be better to stay outside than at home. Actually it's not necessarily the case. But I didn't want to argue. Is it easy in the city? Will there be a future for me in the city? Then I almost hated my parents for pushing me out." Leaving home again, Hua Min felt very disoriented and lost. Feeling she had no place in either the city or the countryside, Hua Min decided to try Shenzhen. When staying in the cheapest hotel for two weeks in this new southern city and having only a few *yuan* left in her pocket, she found a job as a cleaner in a telephone company. The timing turned out to be optimal. At the peak of the bubble economy created by Deng Xiaoping's Southern Tour in 1992, Hua Min was recruited to assist with the expanding sales work in this company and became a sales agent. Before the bubble deflated, she had managed to relocate her household registration from her home village to this city. After Hua Min had a job as a sales agent in Shenzhen, her boyfriend's family, based in Beijing, encouraged the couple to marry. But it was also in Shenzhen where she had one eye seriously and permanently damaged on a sales trip when an elastic strap on her luggage snapped and its mental hook hit her eye. It was in Shenzhen, too, that Hua Min's five-month-old fetus died in her exhausted body, resulting in a difficult abortion and a subsequent three-year Chinese medical treatment. When she was able to conceive again in 1997, Hua Min had to be hospitalized due to the risks involved. Her savings were thus wiped clean and, in 1997, Hua Min once more had nothing. She then moved back to Beijing to be united with her husband and, after her daughter was born, found work in Beijing as a retailer.

Hua Min's sense of migrant rurality grew out of her predicament and hardships. But more than a sense of distress, migrant rurality for Hua Min is also an assertion of an identity with the interests of rural migrant workers and her understanding of the troubles, misery, frustration, and aspirations of her fellow migrants. Her own eight years of experiences as a domestic affirmed what she learned through her native place-based network of *baomu*: "our interests and those of employers are at odds. Employers always would like us to work more, but we hope to work less. Employers would consider you a good *baomu* if you know your position and act by that knowledge, but it is the very position of *baomu* that is oppressive. After eight years of being a *baomu*, I had a very inferior sense of myself and couldn't hold my head up." While in Beijing she associated with women migrants from her own native place, and, after moving on to Shenzhen in 1992 she interacted with many migrants from other provinces whom she encountered on the job. During her five long years of struggles on her own in Shenzhen, the joy Hua Min had was to hang out with other migrants. She liked to hear their stories, to learn where they came from, and to find out what had become of them. She breathed more freely when she was with other migrants. "What will become of our group, the migrant women?" she wondered in the 1990s.

Recent events in her immediate and extended family increasingly troubled Hua Min and pushed her to question the meaning of reform for migrant workers like her siblings, and for the countryside. After working in a beauty parlor in Shenzhen for more than ten years, Hua Min's youngest sister, Hua Xin, had recently quit her job and returned to their native place at the time of our interviews. Ever since I became familiar with Hua Min, she had expressed worries about Hua Xin from time to time, as Hua Xin often complained about headaches and insomnia. "The pressure on her is just too big." Whenever Hua Min spoke on the phone with her, Hua Xin talked about her problems—problems at work and problems with successive boyfriends. Hua Xin had begun to work for the boss of her beauty parlor when she was in her early 20's. At most, her wage was 8000 *yuan* a month. To have a certain security for the future, Hua Xin bought a small apartment in Shezhen. As she grew older, the boss increasingly found fault with her. She did not bring as much profit for the boss as before. But to pay for her mortgage, Hua Xin had to keep her monthly income above a certain minimum. Hua Xin always wished to have a wealthy boyfriend in order to achieve some security. But Hua Min said that Hua Xin could not attain the high and would not settle for the low.

> For more than ten years every day she has associated with rich clients. She identified with their world. But how could wealthy men be seriously interested in a rural migrant woman? Yet she would not be interested in migrant men of her own class, because she looks down upon them and just couldn't see herself as one of them. The older she is, the more anxious she is.

Hua Min worried that her youngest sister might just snap one day, and indeed Hua Xin eventually quit her job. When the boss reduced her wage to only 800 *yuan* a month, one-tenth of what she had earned ten years earlier, she had a fight with her and quit her job. Unemployed and single, Hua Xin in her mid-30s returned to her native place, where she moved in with her other sister, Hua Yu.

Hua Yu lives in the county seat with her two children. Her husband has worked as a salesman for a township and village enterprise (TVE). For a period in the 1980s, when TVEs were doing well, the husband had a good income. So, like prosperous villagers, the family bought an apartment and moved to the county seat. Hua Yu thus quit farm labor and became an urban housewife. But after the mid-1990s TVEs came under stress. Working as a sales representative for one of them, the husband was compelled to spend most of his time in Fujian. During this period, Hua Yu found out that he had found a lover there. Fights ensued and resulted in divorce. Hua Yu is now alone, raising the two children, and has no independent source of income.

Hua Min's parents were very angered by both daughters, especially Hua Xin. They scolded her for being useless and said she brought all her troubles onto herself. Hua Min disagreed, reasoning that the parents were unthinkingly following mainstream values and judgments. "More than ten years working for her boss and my youngest sister was kicked out! 800 *yuan* is basically forcing her to leave." Hua Min's parents now live with her in Beijing. In their old age, the parents are retired from agricultural labor and are reluctant to go back. Some people in the village have been dying of cancer. The lake in the village was contracted to an entrepreneur for fish farming. Now some villagers have flush toilets, which are emptied into the river. Both the lake and river water, which used to be potable, have been badly contaminated. Nobody knows for sure whether the cancer is related to the water's pollution, but people are afraid. Hua Xin reported after a recent trip to the village that it was quite deserted and that some houses, including theirs, were surrounded by overgrown grass. Hua Min would like to persuade her parents to go back and help the two sisters. If the parents could look after Hua Yu's children, then she could search for a job. But Hua Min is not sure whether her parents can be convinced.

Aren't there some in the rural areas who got rich first? In Hua Min's extended family there is one: her own maternal uncle in another village, Li Wei. Li Wei was a migrant construction worker in the 1980s. Rather quickly he turned himself into a contractor (*baogongtou*), recruiting other villagers as migrants for urban construction projects. While the migrants he recruited were paid fixed wages, Li Wei had a flexible income from commissions and became a very rich man. "But out of how many migrants can there be a rich man? How many hundreds of migrants worked hard and were paid no more than a few *yuan* a day, so that my uncle and his family could become rich?!" The uncle is known and disliked by villagers in the surrounding villages. Hua Min's mother used to worry about visits from his family. They would come in cars and make a big fuss. It was not easy to feed and entertain his family.

While still in middle school, Hua Min used to be very fond of and looked forward to Li Wei visits, before he took on the construction work. Her uncle was a very worldly and humorous man. Once he came for a visit and left without staying for a meal. Hua Min very much wanted to stretch his visit longer and ran after him for a long way to urge him to stay. When she finally caught up with him, her uncle gave her one *yuan* and told her to go back. Hua Min bought a pen with that one *yuan*, which she used for the rest of her years in middle and high school. "I have always remembered this experience." But Hua Min noted that years later, when she was a migrant worker in Beijing and heard about her uncle's plan to visit the city, she avoided him. She did not want her uncle to pity her or look down upon her. She also knew she could not offer him help in Beijing. "How different it has become! While before I ran a long way after him to make him stay for a meal, later I tried to stay away from him. My uncle himself doesn't seem to understand why people stay away from him. He wept to my father."

One of Hua Min's cousins recently killed himself by drowning in the village river. The young man, Chen Jiabao, was the only son of her maternal aunt. The aunt and her husband are ordinary peasants and rather poor. Their son worked for Li Wei for a few years in the city. Li Wei and his children had everything, while Jiabao had very little. So Jiabao aspired to be like them. After Jiabao returned to the countryside, he persuaded his parents to give him money to start a business in the city. Several months later he returned, after having squandered his parents' money. He begged his parents again, promising that he would do better this time. His parents did not believe him, but could not ignore his pestering. The poor parents parted with their savings and gave it to him for the last time. Yet he lost it again this time—he was cheated out of his money by swindlers. He was so scared that he did not return to his parents directly, but stayed with his grandparents instead. The grandparents persuaded him to go back and ask for his parents' forgiveness. He went back and knelt in front of his parents. His father was so furious that he told him to get out and that he would not care if he were dead. Jiabao then went to the river. Hua Min was deeply saddened by the community response to his suicidal attempt:

> Some villagers saw him wandering at the bank for quite a while. But no villager tried to pull him back. It's as if people didn't care and were fine with him dead. That's chilling. My aunt and her husband were devastated at the loss of their son. What has become of the countryside?

As related by Hua Min, out of the twenty thousand migrant women from her county who came to Beijing more or less around the same time, two managed to stay on through marriage. The other woman used to nag Hua Min, "People who can manage it try to jump out of the migrant women (*dagongmei*) circle. But you are the opposite: you are always in it." Hua Min relayed this to me and smiled, "I don't know why. I always stand on the position of a migrant woman. Cannot help it." It is her perception of the injustice embedded in her own experiences, in those of her siblings, and in those of many of her migrant friends that have shaped Hua Min's deep identity as a migrant woman, her sense of migrant rurality, and her identification with other migrant workers. For Hua Min to produce her story as a showcase of development would be a betrayal of her critical understanding of her experiences and of the experiences of men and women she has witnessed. She refuses to "stir fry" herself or to be "stir fried." She avoids journalists. She refuses to provide her "voice" to the mainstream society.

Are NGOs Playing Gong Li?: Representation and Ventriloquism

The problem of representation that had troubled Hua Min brings up the question of the subaltern voice. Gayatri Spivak made what seemed a polemical commentary regarding the representation of subaltern consciousness, "the subaltern cannot speak."[4] This provocative but difficult piece of analysis has remained under-appreciated, by and large. Many social scientists find it counter-intuitive since in our field research we surely come into contact with speaking subalterns all the time. Social scientists also find it unsettling, because surely our research papers are filled with voices that we transport back from the field as data. We typically build the validity of our analysis on the basis of the validity and truthfulness of these voices, presuming ourselves to be objective and transparent as we do so.

Is there an objective subaltern voice? Voices of course exist all the time, but they do not exist naturally as pristine data waiting for collection. They are produced in social contexts and in inter-subjective processes. Moreover, they are produced within the frames of the worldviews of the speaker and the investigator. How the speaker understands and interprets his/her situation within what kind of worldview shapes how s/he represents her or his experiences and thus the story told. During the mobilization for land reform and social revolution, poor peasants learned to reinterpret the unfortunate events in their lives in terms of "class" rather than "fate." The act of "speaking bitterness" was not a natural, but a political, process of coming to a consciousness by a performative speaking. When Xi'er at the end of the revolutionary play "White-Haired Girl" was encouraged to speak out against her suffering, she cried out "I'll speak, I'll speak, I will speak!" to a community in transformation. The very possibility of the urge to speak was enabled by a revolution that transformed the local context: the striking down of the local landlord and the imminent land reform that returned land to the tillers. Thus said, speaking in terms of "fate" or "the individual responsible for her self" is nothing natural either, but is a result of long-term everyday socialization. The fact that this process of socialization may be invisible to us does not mean that it is natural. Thus, "speaking" is not a natural or objective process.

The consciousnesses of migrants have mediated relationships with the large structure of political economy, as well as with the complex local histories from which they come. Our analysis thus should not begin with the voice as the given, but should plot the politics of the mediations of their coming to voice. Hua Min's withholding of her voice and Anzi's corporate production of subaltern voice through her migrant workers' club mentioned earlier compel us to question not only whether subalterns can speak, but also—when the popular and academic media endlessly offer us "voices" of the subalterns—how subalterns "speak." Speaking is a socio-political act.

Spivak's polemical commentary calls into question both the essentialist notion of voice and the transparency of both the subaltern speaker and the investigator. The investigator is always a socio-political being. Whenever s/he represents a voice, s/he transposes it into an ideological frame. S/he cannot help it, even though s/he may not be intellectually aware of her or his own ideology. For those who resist this suggestion, James Kavanagh's words in his essay "Ideology" (*Critical Terms for Literary Study*) may be a good reminder: "there is no such thing as a social discourse that is non-ideological…one's insistence that s/he (or a given text) is 'non-ideological' because s/he (or it) disavows any coherent political theory is as silly as would be one's insistence that s/he is 'non-biological' because s/he has no coherent theory of cell formation." [5] However, being "objective" and "non-ideological" is the very value through which mainstream social science establishes its authority in reform China. In the decade of 1990s, "migrant labor" and "migrant population" may be *the* field of social investigation that instrumentally allowed mainstream social science quickly to reshape itself and assert its authority in reform-era China. In this process, data collecting of migrant voices has been a critical exercise of asserting the positivist and objective authority of social science. In the last several years, however, the publications of migrant stories and voices have subtly but fashionably stressed a liberal humanist value of social science. One wonders whether the new attention to and use of migrant voices corresponds with the proliferation of non-governmental organizations (NGO) and the growing NGO funding for social science in China.

Hua Min likes the story of the film "*Qiujudaguansi*" (The Story of Qiuju).[6] She likes to see films about the rural areas, but they are becoming rare these days, even though the majority of the Chinese population is still rural. In the vein of "the subaltern cannot speak," Hua Min protested, "After the film and the sensation, Qiuju is still Qiuju. She is still the rural woman who remains forgotten. It's Gong Li, the actress, who got all the attention and fame." Hua Min's protest gave me pause. As "rural women," "migrant women," and "migrant workers" are increasingly becoming targets for transnational foundations, the number of NGO's claiming to speak for "rural women", "migrant women" and "migrant workers" in China is growing. The demonstrated ability and the act of speaking for these subaltern groups is a critical asset for these NGO's. A conference on migrant women can easily obtain funds in the amount of tens of thousands of *yuan*. Can these groups avoid being Gong Li ventriloquizing Qiuju?

Unceasingly, subterranean experiences keep accumulating. Hua Min's questions of "what will become of us, the migrant women?" and "what has become of the countryside" come from such subterranean experiences. My encountering with Hua Min pushed me to ask: if we are familiar with the logic of GDP accumulation, then what is the trajectory of this subterranean accumulation? What will become of it?

Hairong Yan teaches in the Department of Anthropology, University of Illinois at Urbana-Champaign. She has published in the journals *Cultural Anthropology* and *American Ethnologist*.

---

[1] Lu Xueyi et al. 2002.
[2] For logic of *suzhi* and of self-development and how it has been used to mobilize migrant women, see Yan (2003).
[3] Lu Yao 1995, p. 6.
[4] Spivak 1988.
[5] Kavanagh 1995, p. 311.
[6] Zhang Yimou 1993.

References:

Kavanagh, James. 1995. "Ideology." In Frank Lentriccia and Thomas McLaughlin (eds), *Critical Terms for Literary Study*, pp. 306-320. Chicago: University of Chicago Press.

Lu Yao. 1995. "Ren Sheng." In *Lu Yao xiaoshuo mingzuo xuan* (Selected Well-Known Works of Lu Yao), pp. 1-191. Beijing: Huaxia chubanshe.

Lu Xueyi. 2002. *Dangdai Zhongguo shehui jieceng yanjiu baogao*. (Report on research on present-day Chinese Social Strata.) Beijing: Shehui kexue wenxian chubanshe.

Spivak, Gayatri Chakravorty. 1988. "Can the Subaltern Speak." In C. Nelson and L. Grossberg (eds), *Marxism and the Interpretation of Culture*, pp. 271-313. Urbana and Chicago: University of Illinois Press.

Yan Hairong. 2003. "Neo-Liberal Governmentality and Neo-Humanism: Organizing Value Flow Through Labor Recruitment Agencies." *Cultural Anthropology* 18:4. 493-523.

Zhang Yimou. 1993. Qiuju daguansi (The Story of Qiuju). Beijing dianying xueyuan.

Tales of a Migrant Renovator in Beijing*

Lei Guang

In this article I draw on the story of a migrant home renovator to illustrate the vicissitudes of Chinese reform in general, and the social construction of home renovation (*jiating zhuangxiu* or *jiazhuang* for short) market in Chinese cities since the 1990s. Cheng Gong,[1] my main informant and the hero in this essay, came from a village in Laomei county, Anhui province. He first worked as an itinerant home renovator in Beijing in the early to mid-1990s and then became a micro-entrepreneur with his own small renovation business after 1998. His work experience as a rural migrant in the capital city has coincided with a rapid development of the home renovation industry in the city. Although there is no "typical" migrant experience in China, his life's trajectory as a home renovator brings out several interesting facets of the reform. It not only shows how macro political and socio-economic developments have shaped his life's path, but demonstrates how migrants like him have helped to create the social and economic environment that sustains them in the cities.

Cheng Gong was born in 1974 into an extended family of six that included an aging grandmother, parents, and two other brothers. He earned the envy of the villagers by testing into a very good local high school in 1991, but decided to quit one term before graduation for an apprenticeship with a distant relative-carpenter from a nearby village. His relative took him to Beijing in 1993, and there they started working as itinerant workers in the emerging field of home renovation. He quickly developed a network of friends among his fellow migrants from the same county, but he remained what he calls a guerrilla worker for the first six years. A guerrilla worker, in the context of migratory work in China, refers to someone who has no formal city affiliation, (illegally) solicits customers on the street, and performs it at mobile sites.[2]

Cheng Gong saved some money during those years, but his primary identity was that of an itinerant renovator soliciting work from a makeshift residence. His opportunity came in 1998 when, in response to government encouragement, he and another migrant registered a company under a local "building materials and renovation superstore" in Beijing. In 2001, he registered a higher-grade construction company[3] that allowed him to undertake bigger projects. At the peak of his operation, he had about a dozen teams of five to six migrants each working in the homes (mostly apartments) of Beijing residents. I first interviewed him in 1995, and followed up with additional interviews in 1997, 2002 and 2004. These interviews are supplemented by my observation of him and others at construction sites.

In the following I will first detail a series of national and familial events that led to Cheng Gong's migration from an Anhui village to Beijing. His identity as a market agent is very much shaped by national politics, familial history and, no less, his own conscious choice. In the second part, I will describe his experience as a guerrilla renovation worker in Beijing in the early to mid-1990s. At the time, the home renovation market was thriving under the state's neglect. Many migrants seized the opportunity to eke out a harsh but somewhat profitable living in the city. In the third part of the essay, I focus on Cheng Gong's experience as a budding micro-entrepreneur in the late 1990s and early 2000s. Changing consumer preferences and new government regulations elicited adaptive and transgressive responses from him and other migrant renovators. In this part, I emphasize Cheng Gong's manipulation of the government's effort to formalize the renovation market. I conclude the essay with a discussion of the actually-emerging market as a social convention.

I. The making of a market agent

By Cheng Gong's own account, he was an accidental entrepreneur. His parents are hard-working peasants with little education and no other skills besides being good cultivators of rice, cotton, wheat and vegetables. To them, land is extremely important, and they will go to any length to secure more land for cultivation by the family. His father originally married into his mother's village to help raise her son and to care for an aging mother-in-law from her previous marriage (her former husband died from hepatitis in the early 1970s). Cheng Gong was born shortly after his mother's second marriage in 1974, and a younger brother followed three years later. So on the eve of China's economic reform in 1978, his was a big extended family, with a grandmother, two parents and three boys. In 1983 when he turned nine, his parents decided to move him and his own younger brother back to his father's native village. This move, and the decision to split the extended family into two units, each living in separate villages, was mainly motivated by impending decisions by both villages to divide up the collective land and to contract it to individual households. His father was worried that there would not be enough land to go around for all three boys if they all stayed in one place.

But land was merely an insurance scheme. Like many villagers from the area, his parents had higher hopes that their son would eventually test into a college and become someone who "eats the state-provided grain" (*chi gongjia fan*), i.e., be on the state payroll. Cheng Gong was an excellent student by all accounts; otherwise he would not have gotten into one of the best high schools in the county. But he started high school just around the time when rural education, which had been cheap, was becoming quite costly for cash-strapped peasants. His father's village was much richer than the one they moved from, which only made his household appear poorer in comparison.

Besides, in the early 1990s, more and more village youths began to migrate to the cities, and they brought back cash and alluring tales of city life. Under the circumstances, much to the chagrin of his poor parents, he quit high school in his last year and joined the exodus of villagers for the city. His parents blamed his decision on the bad company he kept in high school. His own explanation was more direct: "for the money and helping out my parents".

> My sole reason for quitting school and becoming a migrant worker was to make money. My purpose is to make enough money so I can help alleviate the poverty of my family. Now I come to think about it, it was pretty feudalistic thinking on my part, because all I wanted then was to help lessen the burden on my parents... I did not give any consideration to myself. I didn't think hard about how to develop myself (*fazhan ziji*) and in which direction. (Interview 3/7/1997)

It did not take long for him, though, to start thinking seriously about his own career in the cities. But he first had to break loose from another "feudalistic" arrangement that tied him to a carpenter-master who was also a relative. Because he was determined to quit school and "to enter society" (*taru shehui*), his parents located a person they could trust to help him: a distant relative from a nearby village who was working as an itinerant carpenter in Beijing at the time. The relative had already worked in Beijing for six to seven years when Cheng Gong was formally introduced to him as an apprentice. The initial agreement was for him to work for the relative for one year in exchange for a bed, meals and one thousand *yuan* at the year's end (the relative was estimated to be making about 20,000 *yuan* a year at the time). After one year was up, the relative wanted to retain him for another year. When he hesitated, the relative threatened to call his parents so that they would "discipline" him. He declined, nevertheless:

> I wanted to leave him after just a half year. By then, I had gotten to know many people so I knew it wasn't difficult to be on one's own. I wanted to work on my own because I wasn't used to being ordered around by someone else. But my Master begged me to stay because he said that I was his first apprentice, and that his reputation would be damaged if I quit in the middle.... Because he was a relative, I decided to stay to finish my one year term... But this was a sacrifice I made for his sake. My relationship to him was not one of partnership, but subordination. (Interview 7/27/1995)

The subtle but palpable change in Cheng Gong's reflections about his familial obligation and his own economic situation in the city illustrates the influence long-distance migration exerts on people. Michael Piore once wrote that migration creates a situation where a migrant's work is divorced from his home social community, so much so that the migrant feels completely uninhibited about pursuing purely economic ends without undue social qualms. "The [migrant] individual's social identity is located in the place of origin, the home community." he pointed out, "The migration to the industrial community and the work performed there is purely instrumental: a means to gather income, income that can be taken back to his or her home community and used to fulfill or enhance his or her role within *that* social structure. From the perspective of the migrant, the work is essentially asocial: It is purely a means to an end. In this sense, the migrant is initially a true economic man, probably the closest thing in real life to the *Homo economicus* of economic theory."[4]

Piore's observation about the migrant as "a true economic man" contains an important element of truth, but it should not be stretched to mean that migrant behavior springs from an innate sense of instrumental rationality and pure economic calculations. As much research on the Chinese rural migrants has shown, village or kin-based networks are an important part of their social world in urban living. More importantly, rural migrants expend much energy in mobilizing social connections at the point of destination in order to seek protection for their employment and/or to advance their careers in the cities.[5]

By the time I first interviewed him in Beijing in 1995, Cheng Gong did not hesitate to call himself a "free" agent in the home renovation market. He felt liberated from relations with his relative-carpenter Master, and he was not obliged to work *for* or *with* anyone else. He was thus free to offer his labor service to Beijing's homeowners. In this sense, he became a *sui generis* economic man in the Piorean sense. But as his brief biography shows, a series of larger events—from his family's initial decision to relocate due to the introduction of the household responsibility system to his migration to his break with the relative wanting to subordinate him—had conspired to shape his life's path toward being a free agent in the marketplace. They made him, and many others, depart from assuming the traditional roles of a village cultivator or becoming a salaried worker in the state sector after college.

II. Working as a guerrilla renovator

According to Cheng Gong and others whom I interviewed, the home renovation industry in Beijing took off in the late 1980s and early 1990s when more and more residents acquired the ownership of apartments under the housing reform. As new urban homeowners poured money into upgrading their once austere-looking apartments, they created work opportunities in old home remodeling and light construction. Most city people disdained unskilled construction jobs, so rural migrants filled the void by supplying home renovation services. In recent years, the urban housing construction boom has also fueled the development of the renovation industry in cities across China. Since home renovation involves customized, small-scale and labor-intensive operation, it was largely neglected by the established state-run construction companies that are more geared toward larger construction projects.

As a result, rural migrants have come to dominate home renovation in almost all cities since the 1980s. For example, many migrant renovators in Beijing came from Anhui, Cheng Gong's native province. When I first interviewed him in 1995, he told me that about two hundred men from his county lived on the same street as he did, and that almost all worked as home renovators for a living. In 2002, he claimed that 60-70% of the migrant renovators in Beijing hailed from his native province, among whom half were from his own Laomei county![6] Renovation-related stories featuring migrant workers and urban homeowners have become popular in city newspapers and on specialized internet sites. In 2004, for example, the Chinese Central Television aired a 20-episode popular TV series, entitled *Carrying Home Renovation to the End*, during the peak spring festival season.[7]

Though mostly involving unskilled labor, home renovation comes at different levels of complexity and is dependent on team work. A simple renovation job may involve just re-painting the walls, adding trims to the wall, or replacing rotting wooden window frames. A more complicated project could entail a remodeling of the kitchen, the installation of a new bathroom, or an overhaul of the plumbing or electrical system in an apartment. Depending on the scale of the project, home renovation could require teams of five or six laborers working together for weeks or even months. The cost to the homeowners could run from several thousand to tens of thousands of *yuan* .

In the 1980s and early 1990s, rural migrants mainly solicited homeowners on the street or by distributing advertisements inside apartment buildings. They were self-styled guerrilla workers. Cheng Gong became a guerrilla worker after breaking free from his Master in 1994:

> We in the home renovation business are 'guerrilla workers' with no fixed place and schedule of work. Everything is good when we have work to do. When we don't have any work, we can't do anything but wait. It is really a matter of luck whether one has work or not. Sometimes, we can't find any work to do for one or two months on end; at other times, we find two

> homeowners [willing to offer us work] in one morning. When I have free time, I usually get out there and distribute flyers. (Interview 3/7/1997)

One of the hallmarks of guerrilla workfare was the irregularity of employment, which was what Cheng Gong had in mind when he referred to his fellow migrant renovators as guerrilla workers. The term also aptly describes their underground status and physical mobility. They were typically not affiliated with any formal construction company, nor were they likely to be registered with the government because of their fear of being identified and repatriated to the villages. They were also physically very mobile because they had to search widely for work and render their labor services in people's homes at multiple sites.

The guerrilla workers were the true pioneers of the renovation market in the city. To advertise their service, they distributed flyers in apartment building and solicited customers on the street. When it came to work, they would typically adopt a flexible arrangement in order to evade government regulations. For example, a group of migrant workers would assemble a team, only *after* one of them had secured a contract. At the end of each job, unless there was more work for them to do, the team members would disband and seek a new combination with others for the next job. Government regulations on registered construction companies thus did not affect them. Their tireless solicitation and flexible services helped to generate a mass demand for renovation among the urban homeowners.

Cheng Gong characterized the home renovation market in his early years as "chaotic" because, as he put it, "the way we competed for work was not regulated." To make their "business" appear legitimate, for example, the guerrilla renovators often solicited work by using the names of fake companies. They would make up the content of advertising flyers to appeal to the urban consumers' sensibilities. Here is one such advertising flyer that Cheng Gong printed and distributed in several apartment buildings in 1995-1996:

Yuanlin Renovation Company, Work First, Pay Later

> *Yuanlin*'s construction department is one of the most trusted enterprises in Beijing. Many years of experience in renovation business. Disciplined workforce with superb skills and craftsmanship. Awarded "Best Enterprise" (*xianjin qiye*) registered with the Beijing Labor Service Company. We now offer work-first-pay-later service (except for institutional clients) in order to better serve our customers and minimize their trouble. We undertake a range of construction projects: institutional buildings, apartments, hotels, restaurants, Kaoroke halls, conference halls, offices, etc. Sample projects and pictures are available for viewing. Free design with latest styles.[8]

The rest of the flyer contained pricing information for labor and materials. A variety of attractive features were added: one-year warranty, 5 percent discount for veterans' families and for people with disabilities, 10 percent discount for people providing leads for other jobs, work on Sundays, etc. Printed in bold were the phone/beeper numbers for contact purposes. The flyer had a nice print layout. It contained enough pricing information for the homeowners so they would feel tempted to make the initial contact.

The *Yuanlin* company never existed, of course. *Yuanlin* was just one of a few nice-sounding names Cheng Gong and others picked up and used alternately with other names at the time (another flyer he was distributing at the time bore the name of *Jingbao* or Beijing Treasure). The information about the company's local history, registration status, and the showcasing of projects was all made up so as to mitigate the urbanite's distrust of outsiders. They made sure their contact number was written in bold. As if all this was not enough, they offered the ultimate assurance to the city residents: we work first, you pay us later.

I cite this example not necessarily to condemn such practices, but to illuminate how information circulating in the home renovation market was generated by the particular social and political dynamics confronting rural migrants in China's cities: they had to disguise the illegality of their service, at least in the first instance, in order to pass muster with urban consumers. Migrants knew that getting the homeowners to talk to them was the most crucial step to securing a contract; so they did not hesitate to serve up fabricated information in the beginning. In the end, these migrant workers had to accept what was dealt them by the market they helped to create, including a price that was acceptable to urban homeowners, and a finished job that was to the latter's satisfaction. They would also want to make sure that, with each completed project, they would gain more social connections in the city that would lead to more work in future.

Reflecting this general social milieu within which renovation work was carried out, the pricing for each renovation project was often a negotiated outcome between the migrants and urban homeowners. The dynamics of demand and supply may have set a broad parameter, but because there were no industry standards either for the migrants or for the urban consumers to follow, the final price tag often depended on the migrants' social judgment and deft negotiation skills.

"We must learn how to judge (*jianbie*) clients in this profession," Cheng Gong explained. He gave me an example when I asked him about the "standard" price he would charge his clients:

> If a client used a cell phone to call me, my initial judgment would be that he is probably generous with his money, or he is relatively well-off. Then I will not give any ground in negotiating the price but will guarantee a top-notch job. People in his position would not trust you if your offer price is too low. Then, there're those who are very frugal with money. They usually call you from a regular phone. They would not use a cell phone even if they had one. You must be flexible on the price when negotiating with such people. Compromise when you have to. Promise a quality job. You make up your loss in the selection of material and style. (Interview 3/7/1997)

Cheng Gong's advantage in this market was his intimate knowledge about the price of building materials and their qualities. The classic situation of information asymmetry gave him some power over his urban clients in negotiating the renovation contract. As I have mentioned, his biggest problem was his outsider status which restricted his legitimate access to the urban home owners. Soliciting them in apartment buildings or on the street could get him into serious trouble with the security guard or the city police. Taking the distribution of flyers as an example, one migrant once told me:

> "There're simply too many restrictions on us passing out flyers. Urban dwellers think too many flyers harm the city image, so the old ladies guarding apartment gates often chase after us. I passed out flyers before, and my targets were dormitories, apartment complexes and tower buildings. I would hold my breath and pray (*tixin diaodang*) while entering the gate, because I did not want the gatekeeper to see me. I would act as if I were a thief. Should they catch me, they would treat me like a thief too." (Interview 7/2/1996)

After the mid-1990s, the central government started to relax some of the restrictions on rural to urban migration, Many large cities, however, retained local restrictions and heavily regulated the migrants' presence..[9] The Beijing municipal government, for example, passed a series of regulations in the mid-1990s that stipulated separate *and* unequal treatment to the migrants in almost every sphere of urban life, from residence permit to work, trade, marriage and birth, education, meals, and lodging standards.[10] For all intents and purposes the rural migrants were excluded from the formal employment market reserved for urban citizens. Owing to their continued exclusion from the urban formal workplace, migrants were monitored by the regular police rather than by their employers or labor officials. In the mid-1990s, the police regularly conducted evening raids in areas where migrants were known to stay at night in order to catch people without proper permits. Many migrants had the experience of being rounded up by the local police and expelled from the city's limits. As Li Zhang has shown in her study of Zhejiang village, entire communities of people could be displaced from their temporary homes in police actions.[11]

Cheng Gong said he was lucky because he was only detained once, in June 1995. It was not long after he started working on his own:

> A fellow worker and I had just gotten off the bus. We were taking a break on the curbside when two plainclothes police approached us and asked for our temporary residence permits. We said we didn't have them on us. They admonished us for not carrying the permits and said we needed to register with the authorities. They then told us to wait inside a van.... Moments later, the van was filled. We were then all taken to a local police station. The room was full of people, and you could see that they were all outsiders.... Because I didn't have any money on me to pay the fine that day, I was sent to a detention camp in Changping for two days... On the third day, a group of us were taken to the railway station and put on a train bound for Suzhou, Anhui province. (Interview 5/19/04)

State control in China was an important factor that shaped its urban labor market in the 1990s. Such control closed off the legitimate avenue for the rural migrants to find formal work in the city. Instead, it forced them underground. State action thus helped to create an informal economic space where guerrilla workers like Cheng Gong thrived. It also served to pattern the interaction between the renovators and their urban customers. The migrants priced their services in accordance with their acute social observations about the urban customers. When necessary, they did not hesitate to serve up “false” information about their business in order to increase their chances of landing yet another new renovation contract.

III. Becoming a migrant micro-entrepreneur

In Beijing, the ineffectiveness of the old administrative method for restricting migration was plain for everyone to see towards the end of the 1990s: the city police and other migrant-control agencies were simply overwhelmed by the influx of rural migrants. Beijing’s regular residents had become quite dependent on all kinds of services provided by the migrants. It was clear that many migrants intended to stay in the city. In this context, the municipal construction authority shifted its tactics from ignoring the large presence of migrant renovators to registering their groupings as government-approved renovation business entities. With the number of renovation-related complaints arising, the municipal authority also began to work on setting quality standards for the industry and on standardizing the contract between homeowners and renovators. The aim was to bring the guerrilla workers above the ground so as to regulate them better.

Against this background, a special committee on home renovation was created under the Beijing Construction and Decoration Association (BCDA, *Beijing shi jianzhu zhuangshi xiehui*) in 1999.[12] The municipal construction authority worked with the committee to propose a number of initiatives aimed at formalizing transactions between renovators and homeowners. Among these initiatives was one that encouraged the establishment of megastores, called home renovation superstores (*jiazhuang shichang*). Such superstores typically occupy a large physical space, integrating many functional areas of home renovation under one roof. In particular, they integrate two key aspects of the home renovation process: the supply of building materials and the provision of renovation services. On one hand, they are gigantic warehouses, much like the Home Depot stores in the US, where all kinds of home construction materials are on display and sold to consumers or construction companies. On the other, they house a large number of registered renovators. For a monthly rent and management fees, the superstores provide the registered renovators with office space, advertise services on behalf of the in-house renovators, and validate contracts between renovators and homeowners.

Around 1998-1999, home renovation superstores began to appear in Beijing and other cities in China. Easyhome (*juran zhijia*), one of the largest construction superstores in Beijing today, opened the first of its four branches in Beijing in March 1999.[13] Like most such superstores, it is jointly owned and controlled by several large state-owned enterprises and private investors who have the capital, the physical space and the local connections to run them. By 2004, there were about forty such superstores scattered around Beijing, with each occupying an area of 20,000 square meters or more.[14] Successful migrant renovators can register their companies in them and solicit work from inside such superstores.

The opening of such superstores marked a turn toward formalization in the management and operation of the home renovation industry after 1999. At the same time, the municipal government and industry associations launched a media campaign exhorting homeowners to use registered renovators. They hoped to end what had appeared to them as haphazard street transactions between guerrilla workers and urban homeowners.

Already a seasoned renovator by the late 1990s, Cheng Gong noticed some subtle but real changes in the demands made by urban consumers. "They became very picky," he said, "At first they asked if you're from a registered (*zhenggui*) or unregistered company. Later, they started quizzing you about the reputation and the size of your company."

> In 1998 we noticed that our clients began to pay attention to the question if we're a registered company [an issue that never arose before]. We realized then that we may not survive long in this field if we do not incorporate our own company... By the end of 1998, seven or eight home renovation superstores had already appeared in the city with hundreds of companies registered with them. (Interview 12/8/2002)

Much like the way that the opening of a Wal-Mart store would reconfigure a locality's retail market dominated by small shop owners, the appearance of such superstores in Beijing altered the rules of the game for the migrant home renovators. The former guerilla workers began to differentiate into two groups: one group of migrants remained unregistered because of a lack of resources, connections or skills. They would face an even harsher market reality than before. The other group of migrants adapted by pooling resources and registered small companies of their own.

Cheng Gong belongs to the latter group. To follow his story, I focus on this latter group of migrant renovators who turned petty entrepreneur in the late 1990s. If the home renovation market I have described in the previous section was constituted by a rather repressive state, unsuspecting urban consumers, and guerrilla workers, the market I am about to depict in this section is one that is shaped by the actions of manipulative urban bureaucrats, including intermediate groups such as the industry associations, critical consumers, and sometimes unscrupulously resourceful entrepreneurs.

Gaining a spot in a home renovation superstore: Cheng Gong made some money doing renovation work in 1997-1998, a time when he began to notice a slight change in the business climate favoring established companies. So, when a fellow migrant worker proposed to him that they form a partnership and register a company, he jumped at such an opportunity. They borrowed someone else's business license and registered a company at a newly-opened home renovation superstore in 1998. After putting down a deposit of 10,000 *yuan*, they started soliciting renovation work from a rented space inside the superstore. Compared to some of the giant stores, theirs is small and a little shabby-looking. It occupies just one floor—about 300 square meters—of an old building once owned by a state construction materials company. The good thing is that the rent is low, about 180 *yuan* per square meter per month. The store management charges a one percent commission on the value of all contracts signed by the renovators.

Business was brisk in the beginning, according to Cheng Gong. "There was a clear increase in both the number of jobs and the value of each project after we registered with the superstore, compared with when we were on the outside," Cheng Gong said. They stopped walking the streets and distributing blind flyers in the apartment complexes now that the customers could find him at his booth in the superstore. But, because of the rent and fees, the cost of providing home renovation service increased. In the down season, the expenses of maintaining a fixed space in the superstore could wipe out all the profits. "After half a year, we made a calculation of our costs and profits. We felt that making money was not any easier now. Home renovation is a complex operation. Construction work is complicated. Competition is tough." (Interview 12/8/02) Indeed, his partner, who had suggested the idea of registering with the superstore in the first place, decided to quit in 2000. He simply went back to work for others rather than run his own business.

Cheng Gong decided to stick with the company because he felt "he could still do it." By then he had gotten to know the superstore management well and begun to socialize with some members of the local branch of the construction and renovation association. He and his partner had to use someone else's business license to register their company in 1998. Since then, the Beijing Industry and Commerce Bureau began to allow non-Beijng residents to apply for their own licenses if they could provide temporary residence permits, a city address and a business account with sufficient funds. So Cheng Gong persuaded the superstore managers to allow him to use the store address to apply for a business license of his own in 2001.

In the meantime, his membership in the local renovation association has helped him to gain some legitimacy in the eyes of increasingly wary consumers. As I have mentioned earlier, Beijing's home renovation association, the BCDA, has played an important role in promoting the industry. It has worked closely with the government to set standards and regulations, and then through its branch associations, helped to channel the information about the new policies and regulations to the members. Since 1997, the BCDA has published a series of pamphlets on the self-regulation of the industry, from samples of renovation contracts, to procedures for resolving the dispute between renovators and consumers, to environmental and quality standards. The BCDA branch associations have held exhibits, sponsored trade shows, and established awards for excellence in home renovation.[15] Realizing the importance of the industry association, Cheng Gong has kept his membership current in the hope of benefiting from his connections with local members. It only helps him that some of the members hold concurrent positions in the government.

Upgrading business certification: Such connections were clearly useful when Cheng Gong decided to upgrade his business certification in 2002. When he registered his company in 2001, it was designated at the "home renovator grade," a special category created just for people like him. The BCDA's home renovation committee created the category in order to formalize the registration of home renovators. However, a problem with this designation is that the home renovator grade is still one level below the lowest grade in the construction industry. While a third-grade construction company, the lowest in the industry, can contract both residential and commercial renovation projects (as long as they cost under 600,000 *yuan*), the home renovator company is not allowed to take on any project larger than residential home renovation. Besides, this special classification begins to lose its cachet among the renovators after some time because any home renovator can receive the special designation by joining the BCDA and paying the membership fee (note: it was 1000 *yuan* in 2004). To distinguish oneself from the rest, a home renovator will want to upgrade to a construction-grade company.

It so happened that, in 2001, the BCDA's committee on home renovation also began to encourage its members to upgrade their certification to the lowest construction grade. This was clearly an attempt to create a hierarchy among the home renovators, and possibly to winnow out small-scale migrant renovators. Setting up a formal home renovation business was already not an easy thing for most migrants; acquiring higher-grade certification was only more difficult for them because of a variety of requirements about their finances, tax status and staffing level. For example, the applicant must have a business account with a deposit of half a million *yuan* or more, a minimum annual revenue of one million *yuan*, and corresponding tax documents. There was simply no way for someone like Cheng Gong to come up with the requisite resources and business papers.

It turned out, however, that none of the above-mentioned requirements was an obstacle for him. He found out that plenty of people and institutions, including public accounting firms, could "handle" such matters for him for a hefty fee. He calls them "certificate handlers" (*banzhao gongsi*). They are not exactly underground operators either, as they openly advertise their services in the newspapers.

His challenge in getting his business upgraded this time pertained to the staffing level. He needed to find fifteen "staff persons" with a variety of professional certificates: construction engineers, accountants, designers, and building inspectors, etc. The registration bureau normally accepted the photocopies of ID's and diplomas, which would have been easy to forge. But since the bureau designated the year of his application (2002) as the year of e-government or office computerization, the officials demanded the submission of *both* the originals and the duplicates of all the staff persons' certificates. They needed the originals for scanning, and the duplicates for paper records. Since this was a city-wide operation, it was near impossible for Cheng Gong to "borrow" so many ID's and diplomas at the same time, as others also needed them. He managed to collect the documents from eight retired professionals in 2002, but with that he all but exhausted his acquaintances who could help him. Betting on an easier registration process the next year, he pleaded with some association members to intervene on his behalf and have the registration bureau issue a *temporary* license that would be subject to review one year later. In 2003, he was able to collect enough ID's and diplomas and successfully converted his temporary license into a permanent one. Again, he sought help from some members of the local home renovation association. In exchange, he paid 10,000 *yuan* to support local association activities.

Dealing with critical consumers: Cheng Gong had no way of predicting, however, if his money was well spent when he applied to upgrade the license of his company from the home renovator to the construction grade. Beijing's home renovation industry had grown by 26 percent on average each year from 1998 to 2002, so he was betting on its continued growth. As of 2005, the director of the BCDA had estimated that half a million Beijing residents renovate their houses or apartments each year.[16]

For individual renovators, an increase in the aggregate demand does not always translate into more business. In recent years, urban residents have become more critical consumers of home renovation services. They have not only become more conscious about the cost, but grow wary about fraudulent companies using poor-quality and even hazardous construction materials, or simply not following through with the original design. Considerations of cost and concerns about quality alternately compel them to seek out guerrilla workers and registered renovators. To be successful, home renovators like Cheng Gong have to adapt constantly to shifting consumer preferences and to develop new business strategies.

Chinese urban residents seeking to renovate their homes had four main ways of finding a renovator in the early 2000s. First, there were still the guerrilla workers, whom they could meet on the street or call by using the phone numbers printed on hand-distributed flyers. By that time, many residents distrusted guerrilla workers because of the negative publicity they had received in the media and because of the governmental campaign against them. The proportion of unregistered and mobile renovators may have decreased somewhat, but they still make up a significant part of the renovation workforce in Beijing, as in other cities across China. A conservative estimate is that unregistered guerrilla renovators still accounted for about 40 percent of the renovation market share in Beijing in 2004.[17]

The second means of locating a renovator was by visiting various renovation superstores to contract with their in-house renovators. Government regulators encourage city residents to pursue this option, as do the industry associations that are dominated by representatives from the superstores. But Cheng Gong has observed a decline in the popularity of in-house renovators among consumers after 2000. Fewer and fewer home-owners pay visits to the renovators inside these stores because the latter tend to charge a significantly higher price than do those who are not affiliated.

A third way for urban homeowners to find a suitable renovator was to thumb through the printed ads pages of city newspapers. Cheng Gong discovered that newspaper advertisement gained momentum soon after he had set up a booth in the superstore. Many low-priced and seemingly trustworthy companies eschewed expensive superstores by taking their ads directly to the newspapers. Gone are the days when migrant renovators had to rely on small street vendors for printing flyers; city newspapers now vie with each other for their advertisement business. For awhile, newspaper advertisement was the most favored venue for publicizing renovation services. In 2001, home renovation was one of the three most heavily advertised areas in Beijing's newspapers, after automobiles and real estate. Cheng Gong himself started advertising in several newspapers in 2002. When I talked to him in 2004, however, he was reducing the amount of his advertising in newspapers. It seemed that the flood of newspaper ads created a confidence gap among the consumers about the veracity of their contents.

Finally, by 2004, many consumers seemed to have returned to the old-fashioned method of visiting on-site renovation companies and checking out model apartments. When Cheng Gong started to cut back on newspaper advertisement in 2003, he embarked on a new strategy for soliciting work in new apartment complexes. He calls it the "inside-community" strategy (*xia xiaoqu zhanlue*). The idea is to move groups of workers to a newly-completed apartment building before the residents have made up their mind about renovation. The renovators will rent an apartment, set up a temporary office, and then invite the occupants to come to the office next door for a look at pictures of old models or new designs. The inside-community strategy certainly makes it convenient for homeowners to find renovation workers. Face-to-face interaction on the premises also reduces the residents' distrust of foot-loose renovators.

But there were a number of disadvantages to this fourth strategy. It worked only in the case of newly-completed apartment complexes, where there was a concentrated demand for renovation services in a short period of time. Physically locating oneself in one apartment building, however temporarily, mostly limited one's contacts to the neighbors in that one community. There was also the cost associated with setting up a temporary on-site office. More than one renovation company may move in at the same time so the competition is still strong. As has happened many times for Cheng Gong, migrant renovators had to obtain approval from the building managers, or bribe them for access.

When I last interviewed Cheng Gong in May 2004, he had stopped soliciting work on the street and all but ended newspaper advertisements. He still kept a small office in a decrepit superstore, but that was mainly for the purpose of maintaining ties with the store's managers. He sent almost all his workers to various on-site offices in newly-finished apartment complexes. He was not optimistic that this new strategy will be viable in the long run. As he put it, the change in the renovation market "has not been as smooth as I anticipated."

Sub-contracting against government rules: To combat the vagaries of a shifting market, Cheng Gong has adopted subcontracting as the main method of organizing work. This is reminiscent of his guerrilla worker days. Government policies forbid the subcontracting of work to smaller, independently-run construction teams: those who contract the work must perform it, according to government rules. Only the big developers and high-grade construction companies are allowed to subcontract work to lower level firms (*zhuanbao*) or divide the work with a third party (*fenbao*).

In actuality, most home renovators do not follow these rules. They practice all kinds of subcontracting arrangements, especially when they are busy and need more hands. Even in the case of guerrilla renovators, the person who contracts the work is not necessarily the one who does it: he is likely to contract it to others so he can focus on getting the next job. Several migrants told me that they *specialize* in getting the renovation jobs and give them to others to finish. All they need for the purpose of work are a phone line (or beeper in the old days), congenial manners, and good communication skills.

Cheng Gong himself specialized in "getting jobs" for his fellow migrants towards the end of his career as a guerrilla worker. After registering his own company, he seemed to follow the same practice of contracting out most of the renovation work in spite of government policies. As he explained to me, the subcontracting system now operates in this way: a regular staff member of his company, a "solicitor" (*zhaohuode*), approaches a prospective customer and engages him or her to learn the extent to which he or she is willing to sit down and talk about his or her renovation needs. The solicitor then passes the customer to a "negotiator" (*tanhuode*) who then explains the renovation process and engages in preliminary negotiations over the price. The "negotiator" is a key person who remains an important mediator between the company, the construction workers, and the customer. If the customer is willing to proceed at this point, a designer (*shejishi*) will be called in to explain the various design and price options. All the work up to that point is done by a core group of people who are likely to be the only "permanent" employees of the company. After the customer agrees on a price and a plan, Cheng Gong then contacts one of the supervisors of construction workers. He works out an agreement with the supervisor and pays him a lump sum for the construction work. Since the supervisor may be the head of more than one team of workers, he often sub-contracts work to another member of the team. The designated worker acts as the temporary supervisor, who then organizes all the construction work on the site.

From Cheng Gong's vantage point, the whole arrangement looks like a pyramid with him on the top and others bound to him by a chain of responsibility relations. The system not only distributes work, but pushes responsibility and financial risks down to the members of the construction team. One cannot help but draw a comparison with the rural responsibility system with respect to agricultural production. When a client is not satisfied with the final outcome and refuses to pay the full amount, the money lost is usually not absorbed by the company alone, but redistributed at every level of the subcontracting chain. The system also allows for risk-sharing when accidents happen. As of 2004, Cheng Gong had not bought any outside insurance for his workers. He claimed to follow an "internal" insurance strategy, whereby the responsibilities (and liabilities) are shared by everyone at each level of the subcontracting relations. "I shift some of the liabilities to the supervisor, and the supervisor in turn shifts some onto the workers," he stated, as he aptly summed up another aspect of the subcontracting system.

Adapting to the dramatic growth in Beijing's home renovation market in the late 1990s, rural migrants like Cheng Gong brought their underground business out into the open and started soliciting work as registered renovators. As in the 1980s and early 1990s, their participation in Beijing's growing renovation industry has shaped who provides what kinds of renovation service to Beijing residents, and via which venue. Through ingenuity and manipulation, migrant renovators like Cheng Gong have not only gained "legitimate" access to renovation work in Beijing, they have also proven to be quite able to adapt to changing consumer trends by altering the venues they use in soliciting home-owners and by organizing work in a pyramid structure of subcontracting relations. Beijing's home renovation market, as it continued to boom throughout the 1990s, was shaped by the interaction of more permissive state policies, resourceful rural renovators, and critical urban resident-consumers.

Conclusion

Through the story of Cheng Gong's odyssey in Beijing, I seek to describe the economic and socio-political dynamics that have shaped his life's path from an uninitiated village youth to a seasoned migrant renovator in the city. In the process, Cheng Gong has fashioned himself into an active agent in the market who, along with millions of other migrants, helped to create a booming renovation market in Beijing as well as in other cities in China. He was not born a "free" agent of the market, but a series of national and familial events steered him in that direction in the 1980s and early 1990s. Since then, he has learned to live with and adapt to the changing market conditions in a thriving industry in urban China. Cheng Gong and his fellow migrants are no passive learners. Their creativity, deception and manipulation actively shaped the contours of the actually-emerging home renovation market, under conditions created by shifting collective preferences of urban consumers, and by the various government regulations, including those that once denied them the right to work in the cities.

Lei Guang is an Associate Professor of political science at San Diego State University. His articles have appeared in such journals as *Politics & Society, International Migration Review, Modern China, China Quarterly, Critical Asian Studies, Pacific Review*, and positions.

---

* An earlier version of the paper was presented at the "Narratives of Reform" workshop at University of California-Irvine on May 22, 2004. The author acknowledges the support of a Faculty Development Grant from the San Diego State University 2003-2004. Thanks to Deborah Davis, Mark Selden, and especially, Dorothy Solinger for comments on previous versions of the paper.

[1] To disguise the identity of the interviewee, I have altered some minor details in his biography, including the name.
[2] For more on the guerrilla workers, see Guang, 2005.
[3] According to my interviewee, construction companies are graded into three levels (one being the highest grade and three being the lowest) and certified by the local construction authorities under the Ministry of Construction. Home renovation is a relatively new area, and most renovation companies are registered at the sub-construction grade level. A higher-grade registration, if it can be obtained, lends more prestige to the company and thus allows the company to charge higher prices than a lower-grade renovation company.
[4] Piore, 54.
[5] See Guang.
[6] There is no reliable statistics on the number of migrant renovators. These figures given by Cheng Gong may well be an exaggeration, but they underscore the significant presence of rural Anhui migrants in this growing industry.
[7] The popular TV series, entitled in Chinese "*Jiang jiazhuang jinxing daodi* (Carry Home Renovation to the End), was directed by Han Weiping, and started to air on the Chinese New Year's Day in 2004. It starred Xu Gehui, a popular TV personality in China, and Fan Wei among other popular actors and actresses.
[8] Name and phone numbers are crossed out in order to protect the anonymity of my informant.
[9] Zhang, 46.
[10] Beijing shi.
[11] Zhang.
[12] See http://www.bcda.com.cn/gyxh/jjwyhzc.asp for documents on the establishment of the home renovation committee in 1999. Accessed on May 1, 2005.
[13] See brief history of Easyhome in Beijing, http://www.juran.com.cn/docc/gsgk1.asp. Its northern branch on the outer No. 4 ring road boasted retail space of 56,000 square meters and sales revenue of 1.5 billion yuan in 2002. Accessed on May 1, 2005.
[14] See Zhu.
[15] See the Association's website, http://www.bcda.com.cn/, for more information on the range of activities it sponsors. Accessed on May 1, 2005.
[16] See http://www.bcda.com.cn/gyxh/jjwyhzc.asp, and Zhu Xibin, "Jiazhuang jiancai hangye"
[17] "Zhenggui zhuangshi shigong qiye zuo jiaju zhuangshi zhuangxiu de shichang fen'e yijing dadao 60% yi shang" *Beijing jiating zhuangshi* [Beijing home renovation], no. 15 (2003): 15.

References:

Beijing shi laodong ju (Beijing labor bureau). *Waidi Laijing Renyuan Guanli Shiyong Shouce* (Practical guide to the management of migrant workers in Beijing), Beijing: Beijing shi laodongju bianyin, 1995.

Block, Fred. "Karl Polanyi and the Writing of *the Great Transformation.*" *Theory and Society* 32 (2003): 275-306.

Granovetter, Mark. "Economic Action and Social Structure: The Problem of Embeddedness." *American Journal of Sociology* 91, no. 3 (1985): 481-510.

Guang, Lei. "Guerrilla Workfare: Migrant Renovators, State Power and Informal Work in Urban China." *Politics & Society*, 33, no. 3 (2005): 481-506.

Piore, Michael J. *Birds of Passage: Migrant Labor and Industrial Societies*. Cambridge: Cambridge University Press, 1979.

Solinger, Dorothy. *Contesting Citizenship in Urban China.* Berkeley: University of California Press, 1999.

Zhang, Li. *Strangers in the City*. Stanford: Stanford University Press, 2001.

"Zhenggui zhuangshi shigong qiye zuo jiaju zhuangshi zhuangxiu de shichang fen'e yijing dadao 60% yi shang" (Market share of registered renovation companies has increased to over 60%), *Beijing jiating zhuangshi* [Beijing home renovation], no. 15 (2003): 15.

Zhu Xibin, "Jiazhuang jiancai hangye shichang fazhan yu meiti chuanbo zuoyong yu zeren tantao" (Exploration of the role and responsibilities of media in the development of home renovation materials market), (http://news.soufun.com/detail.html?newsid=322698, accessed on January 20, 2005)

The Story of Secretary Wang – Hero, Savior, Liar, Scoundrel*

Tim Oakes

It's a typical day for secretary Wang.[1] He's walking through the village, with a group of visitors in tow. They're students this time, from the local technical school on a Sunday outing. Wang is in his element, doing what he does best. His well-practiced narrative echoes through the tightly-walled lanes of the village. "...And up here is one of our finest *menzhao*," he says, stopping beneath an ornately carved and elaborate doorway leading into one of the village's many courtyard houses. "Before liberation," he continues after the group gathers outside the doorway, "this was a very cultured village. Over one third of the households were landlords! The door to one's home is like one's face; it symbolizes your status and wealth just like those luxurious reception rooms people put in their modern apartments today. These days..." But suddenly Wang's mobile goes off, playing its familiar little jingle. "Wei!" he shouts into it, and then rattles off something in rapid local dialect that I can't understand. This is part of the tour as well. I've never seen Wang get through a tour without his phone going off at least three or four times.

He slaps the mobile shut and shoves it in his pocket. "Let's see... where was I? Oh yes – these days Jiang Zemin and Deng Xiaoping consider the landlords the advanced representatives of economic progress. We should understand this. To me, they weren't landlords, they weren't exploiters. They were people who worked hard, saved their money, and advanced the village along with themselves." It's almost eerie when Wang says this, because he could easily be talking about himself. He *is* talking about himself, as he follows in his ancestors' footsteps through the lanes and courtyard houses of the village. Secretary Wang is the new landlord of Niuchangtun, a village in Guizhou province.[2] He knows it. And everyone else in the village knows it. But his wealth is not land. What Wang holds a monopoly on is something much more sophisticated and valuable. He owns the culture and heritage of his village. And he has turned these into a very profitable business for himself, "advancing the village along with himself."

I first met Wang in 2002. A local scholar was showing me some of the villages where he'd been doing research for the past decade. I was looking at the area as the potential site for a new project on Guizhou's Tunpu culture revival. That was when I first got Wang's tour. We had lunch at his house, after which he pulled out various newspaper articles and stories that had been written about him. I started to become familiar with his history through what others had written about him. They all told the story of a model worker, one who had endured every hardship in his struggle for the betterment of his village and himself. He's an example for all of China's country folk to learn from. I started to see Wang as both a sort of gatekeeper for my own project, as well as a compelling individual in his own right. I needed to learn more about him.

About a year later—in November, 2003—I interviewed him for the first time as I was doing reconnaissance work for potential field sites. After the project got underway, repeated interviews were conducted in 2004 and 2005. While doing fieldwork in Niuchangtun, I often stay at Wang's house, eating with his family, interviewing him and interviewing other villagers about him. We have gotten to know each other through my repeated visits. Wang cultivates our relationship because of my potential role as a consultant and promoter of his village's tourism development. And I cultivate our relationship because of his pivotal role in his village's development and because I now hold the idealistic and perhaps naïve belief that my work with Wang will ultimately make life better for everyone in Niuchangtun.

This chapter attempts to tell three stories simultaneously. One story is simply a biography of one of China's millions of intelligent, dynamic, and driven peasants, one who has managed to navigate the twists, turns, and pitfalls of China's socialist (and now capitalist) modernization, and managed somehow to come out near the top of the heap. The experience has scarred Wang, both physically and mentally. Yet he forges ahead with admirable pluck and enviable ambition.

Another story seeks to tell what happens when China's new economy of culture and leisure (Wang 2001) reaches the villages. What happens when a villager like Wang is confronted with the possibilities of a new regime of capital accumulation based on "culture?" What happens when an abstract and foreign concept like "culture" descends on a village with the promise of leading people out of poverty and giving them a newfound sense of prestige? Wang has been adept at grasping the potential of culture as a means of enriching both himself and his village, but his enthusiasm is not shared by all of his neighbors, and his talents for cultural promotion have come at the cost of alienating many of his fellow villagers.

The third story is more personal and reflexive. It is about what happens when a research project studying this process *also* descends on a village? What happens when the process of change you come to study is itself shaped by the fact that you have come to study it? It was my intention all along to develop a research project that would—through the practice of fieldwork itself—help guide tourism development toward more sustainable outcomes. Nevertheless, I find myself caught between a researcher's fascination with his subject and an activist's desire for intervention. And this is why my relationship with Wang is both so important and so difficult. He is both the primary agent of change through which my research might have a direct impact on Niuchangtun, and yet I also see him as one of the key obstacles to the kinds of changes that I have come to feel are necessary if Niuchangtun is to benefit, collectively, from tourism. My hope remains that our relationship will eventually enable a common vision to emerge in which we can both feel equally invested.

The chapter thus narrates a moment in a research project that is not yet complete, and it tells a story that is ongoing. It is, in that sense, a very preliminary sketch of a history that continues to unfold.

Wang was born in 1943. He comes from a family of craftsmen. Weavers. A "petty-bourgeois" class background. When land reform was carried out seven years later, this by itself was not a damning class background. But Wang's father had been a Guomindang official; he had been mayor of the local township. And despite the fact that his father had been shot dead by bandits when Wang was only three years old (not an uncommon occurrence in those days), his association with counterrevolutionaries weighed heavily against Wang's family. Today Wang calls his father a Guomindang "collaborationist" who was forced into public service by virtue of the family's inability to support itself through textile production.

Wang was the fourth of seven children. "A family of four daughters," he says, shaking his head. "It was very hard for my mother. After my father's death, we were very poor," he says. "She had to support the whole family with her weaving and making tofu." His older brothers were able to work, however, and soon Wang was able to work too. He would have preferred school. He started attending classes at age 11 and excelled immediately, was even recognized with "student cadre" status as a result. Four years later, though, the village was thrown into the Great Leap Forward.[3] Wang's school was closed after villagers were mobilized to dig coal mines, cut down trees, smelt steel, and construct dams. He was 15 years old and, in the chaos of those years roamed freely, finding in the cracks of rapid collectivization in the countryside opportunities to make money. Today Wang expresses no regrets over this key moment in his life, when the potential for the life of an intellectual was eclipsed by that of a shrewd and calculating businessman. Nor has the value of an education been something that Wang has sought to impart to his own children. He has not hesitated to take his son out of school so that the boy can accompany him on business trips or pursue other kinds of work to enhance the family income.

By the early 1960s, Wang was traveling back and forth between Guizhou and Sichuan, selling tobacco in Chongqing and Chengdu, and buying cotton yarn in those cities to sell back in Guizhou, all for a tidy profit. It was easy money. "Back then," he says, "there were free markets everywhere. The opportunities for making money were endless for anyone willing to suffer a little." People could go into business as much as they wanted. The markets were especially big in Sichuan, he said. But he returned to the village in 1963 and, curiously, started working at a nearby hydroelectric station. It's moves like this which illustrate the political savvy that complements Wang's business savvy. Whether he sensed the political storm that was just gathering over the horizon, or whether he simply felt that more stable employment was a good idea, is hard to say. But the move gave Wang a shelter of sorts during the early years of the Cultural Revolution. By 1965 his intelligence got him promoted to the propaganda department. He was 22 years old, and, for the first time in his life began to think that he had a truly promising future in front of him. He even managed to join the Communist Youth League, a feat which still today he compares to "ascending heaven," given his father's status as a "collaborator."

His unexpected tenure of political correctness was not to last, however. Within a year he had been sacked, a victim of the Cleansing of the Class Ranks campaign. The entire hydroelectric bureau, by virtue of its connection to the center, then came under attack by Red Guards. "They came out to the hydro station, called us all capitalist roaders. They marched me around with an ox-head placard. I had to leave the station." Wang returned home, and though most people in his situation would have been expected to lay low and keep out of trouble, Wang went back to plying his old trade routes, finding spaces for business opportunity hidden within the chaos of the Cultural Revolution.

Whether his family's poverty compelled him to do this he won't say. But I'm tempted to believe that he was astute enough to recognize the risks he was taking. In fact, it turned out not to be worth the risk. Wang was arrested in 1972 and charged with profiteering. He spent three years in jail, and another three years in a labor camp.

In 1978 he was released and returned to his village. He immediately started sojourning again. His family pleaded with him to stay in the village but he wouldn't listen. He collected crude pottery from villages and sold it in the provincial capital. He even sold paintings that he himself made. He sold anything he could get his hands on. He drifted around the country for a couple years. He went to Wenzhou, bought fake Rolex watches and sold them in Guizhou for a nice profit. He also went to Liangshan in Sichuan and bought silver jewelry from the Yi people, which he sold in Guangzhou. "In 45 days I made over 40,000 yuan," he said of the silver trading. This money gave him a basis from which to reestablish himself in the village. Wang is one of those people who is not fooled into making money for its own sake; he understands that money itself is unimportant unless it can be exchanged for power.

The way he puts it today, he was wandering about China when he heard the news of the 1978 Third Plenum of the Eleventh Central Committee, that pivotal meeting of Party leaders in which Deng Xiaoping emerged, unopposed, to proclaim a new course for a country weary of political turmoil. The news struck him as an important opportunity and he decided to return to the village and invent a new life for himself, as village leader.

It's not easy to believe Wang when he says this. It is unlikely that anyone, at the time, really recognized the significance that the Third Plenum would ultimately have. While the meeting clearly indicated that change was afoot, no one then knew what that change meant or where it would lead.[4] It is unlikely that the leadership itself understood the significance of the moment until the reform agenda became solidified over the next several years and an orthodox history of the reforms then underway could begin to be written. But Wang's reinvention of this moment is still revealing of a mind that has been able to adapt that orthodoxy to his own life story remarkably well. This ability to reinvent his life so that it aligns with the trajectories of power that continue to reshape China at a national or regional scale is something that Wang displays again and again when narrating the story of his life. It is also apparent from his current actions as leader of a village seeking to promote itself to tourists. But here I am jumping ahead of the narrative.

Power is something with which Wang is familiar in other ways too. For it is true, as he says during the tours he gives of his village, that over a third of its residents were landlords. Before liberation, Niuchangtun was not a village of farmers. Those who weren't outright landlords were typically engaged in some sort of trade. Mao may have turned them into farmers, but they maintained an identity as *kejia*, "guest families" literally. In this region of Guizhou, *kejia* are known as people who came to the province to set up businesses following the initial waves of military colonization during the early years of the Ming Dynasty. They had specialized skills and typically regarded themselves as more civilized than their fellow frontiersmen. Wang articulates an identity as *kejia* when he tries to explain the underlying reasons for his success. It is as if his business sense runs in his blood. Farming was simply never an option for him. He is *kejia*. He does business.

So, in 1983 he returned to the village, loaded with cash, and started a public welfare group (*gongyi xiaozu*) to help the poorer villagers. I see this as both a genuine effort to help those who were less able to benefit from the early reforms, and a calculated strategy to rehabilitate himself and position himself to gain power in the village. Wang is like that, he's both compassionate and willing to step on people who get in his way. He knew that the decollectivization campaign then in progress to dismantle the communes would require an entirely new administrative system, and he was shrewd enough to position himself politically in anticipation of the change. And sure enough, by 1984 he had been selected village head, with the help of relationships with local officials he had cultivated. Other villagers say he "bought" his appointment, with gifts and other favors to the local officials who oversaw the transformation from commune brigade to administrative village that occurred nationwide in those years. Today, others in the village say that Wang would never have been approved by the higher ups—because of his family's bad class background—if not for his bribery. But these are claims made twenty years after the fact, during a time when Wang's leadership has alienated many in the village. Back in 1984 Wang was the only one in Niuchangtun with both a vision for achieving prosperity and the cash to turn that vision into a reality. It clearly made him the obvious choice to lead the village into the reform era. Like so many others persecuted during the Cultural Revolution, the fact that Wang had done hard time in the 1970s gave his reformist credentials a stamp of authenticity that others could not match.

His first act was to clean up the village. He started a campaign to earn "civilized" status for Niuchangtun, which indeed was granted the following year, in 1985. He sponsored outdoor movies as a way of gathering villagers together to entreat them to clean up the streets and alleyways, and wash their houses. He also aggressively pursued contracts with nearby urban businesses, creating putting-out systems in the village for textiles and other craft products. By 1986 his successes were being noticed by the province and Niuchangtun was recognized as a model village. Wang was being invited to attend conferences and workshops on economic development. *Guizhou Daily* sent one of its best reporters to stay in Niuchangtun for two weeks. This journalist wrote a front page article about Wang, which was also featured in propaganda reports sent to other provinces. Wang says that people started to come from all over China to see the village and learn about how it was so quickly recognized as a civilized and model village. "They came from as far away as Xinjiang, Gansu, Fujian," he said. "This was the first time outsiders of any importance had ever been to the village." His work not only brought outsiders to Niuchangtun, but more importantly cemented the village's celebrity image in the eyes of local officials. A few years later, when economic development strategies started to emphasize tourism, local officials naturally saw Niuchangtun as a likely target for development. And while much of rural China was witnessing the gradual rollback of many of the gains in living standards brought by the first wave of reform in the early 1980s (see Unger and Xiong 1990; Croll 1994), Niuchangtun saw steady improvement through the latter half of the decade. And Wang, of course, was doing well for himself too. He had opened his own coal mine—technically a Township and Village Enterprise—but it was basically his own business. It remains a sore point for some of the other villagers even today, the first case of Wang really using his official position for personal enrichment.

But in 1992 he was severely burned in a fire. It should surprise no one that the fire was in a fireworks factory. Such fires have claimed the lives of thousands throughout China. Wang claims that his burns were due to his heroisms—saving others instead of himself. It's a good example of my difficulty with Wang. On the one hand, he is a tireless worker, very smart, someone who has sacrificed for his village. On the other hand, this applies equally to his abilities for self-promotion and personal enrichment. I find myself admiring and despising him at the same time. His burns were severe. His hands were burned so badly that he now has mangled stubs instead of fingers. He can use them just enough to hold a pair of chopsticks or his ever-chiming mobile phone. His face was disfigured. He lost all his hair and now wears a toupee which is badly in need of replacement. He spent years recovering, hooked on pain-killing drugs. He says the government didn't provide any support for his family during this time, and he grew disillusioned. And it's easy to say that many people would have just given up at this point. But not Wang.

In 1997 he left the village for Kunming. His son quit school and went with him. Wang did not intend to return. He was broken and bitter. Clearly he felt that he was owed something by the village, but it remains unclear why he left. It's one of those rare periods of his life that he refuses to reinvent. He does say that it was the lowest point in his life, that he cared for no one but himself. It is likely that after spending years recovering in the hospital he was simply out of money and needed to return to sojourning. Before he left, however, he did manage to build a new house for his family – not the kind of thing done by someone lost in the depths of despair. But throughout his life Wang had responded to hardship and uncertainty by returning to the road, and returning to the business of buying and selling. So here he was again, this time selling fruit on the streets of Kunming.

Suddenly his circumstances changed. In 2000, he says, some of the villagers went to bring him back. They claimed Niuchangtun was adrift without him and that they would support him if he returned to be village head once again. He agreed. Business was poor in Kunming; the money was no longer so easy, and he was getting older.

As fate would have it, his return coincided with the development of a new economic opportunity for Niuchangtun: the rise of Tunpu "culture fever." He wasted no time in campaigning for the village's recognition as an "open air museum" of Tunpu culture.

"Tunpu" is a new label used by local scholars, officials, and, increasingly, villagers themselves, for those descendents of early Ming soldier-colonists sent to pacify the frontiers and conquer Yunnan. While many throughout Guizhou can claim ancestry dating to the large influx of population that occurred in the late 14th century, Tunpu people are said to have maintained a unique set of cultural practices that have changed little over the ensuing 600 years. In the 1980s, local scholars started seeing in many of the Tunpu villages patterns of dress, language, ritual, and architecture dating to the early Ming. And because the early Ming was *the* formative period for Guizhou as a province (officially founded shortly after the Ming colonization, in 1413), Tunpu people have become the symbolic inheritors of Guizhou's distinctive heritage. Today, Tunpu culture is not only the subject of a great many academic books and research articles, but also the subject of many articles in popular magazines, television documentaries, and travel programs. The second-best selling book in Guiyang bookstores in 2004 was titled *Six Hundred Years of Tunpu*, by two well-known local journalists (Yan and Gao

2002).[5] And Tunpu is the focus of the drive to promote cultural tourism in central Guizhou, with at least one village having been turned into a pay-at-the-gate theme park as a result.

One of the most interesting things about Tunpu culture is the way that villagers themselves have come to understand it. While most were usually aware that their ancestors came from other parts of China many centuries ago, and most were even aware that their ancestors were soldiers sent by the first Ming emperor, Zhu Yuanzhang, to pacify and colonize the frontier, few regarded these facts as anything exceptional until local scholars started expressing their amazement at how well the villagers had preserved the traditions of their ancestors. And while the significance of this may have still escaped the villagers, the potential for a new source of income—heritage tourism—did not. Many villagers were quick to grasp the commercial potential of the cultural resources that scholars were claiming villagers possessed. And one of the quickest to grasp this potential was Wang.

As Wang tells it, way back in the 1980s, around the time his village was given "civilized village" status, he realized that the villagers should preserve all those traditional courtyard houses left behind by their landlord ancestors. This is another example of Wang's ability to align his own personal history with the dominant trajectories of power swirling around him. While it's hard to believe that Wang himself was able to see the heritage potential of his village at such an early date (though it may in fact be true), what's most interesting is the fact that—true or not—Wang's personal history has merged with the broader history of reforms. His personal narrative—in his claim to have anticipated the growing culture and leisure economy of the 1990s—parallels the history China's rapidly changing political economy. Wang thus presents himself as a kind of spokesman not only for his village and his people but for the correctness of the reform trajectory. Wang's oral history is by now so wrapped up in the rhetoric of his village tour that his own past and that of the village have become one and the same story.

Wang's village is now one of the recognized icons of Tunpu culture, primarily because of its magnificent architecture. The landlords of Niuchangtun left a tightly packed village of courtyard houses that at once remind one of old villages in Anhui or Zhejiang and, simultaneously of frontier military fortresses. Tunpu's appeal comes in part from its unexpectedness in a place like Guizhou, so far from those regions of China where one expects to find courtyard homes. Most of Guizhou's rural landscape is either too poor to have generated the kind of wealth to build such homes, or it is inhabited by minorities, for whom courtyard homes are not a typical architectural custom. But the ancestors of the Tunpu were from the downriver regions of old money—southern Anhui, northern Jiangxi, Zhejiang—where courtyard homes were common, and they were later joined by merchants who built more ornate and luxurious homes than the fortress-hybrids constructed by the colonizing soldiers. Niuchangtun is one of those villages of later arrivals—the *kejia*—dating only to the mid to late Qing Dynasty, and thus features the more elaborate version of Tunpu courtyard architecture.

In the 1980s, the local government started to promote Tunpu culture for tourism development, but Tunpu remained more of an intellectual project than anything until 2001, when Beijing recognized Niuchangtun and seven neighboring villages for state-level heritage protection status. Wang was a key figure in generating local support for heritage status among the villagers. He says he came up with the idea of preserving his village's landscape back in 1985, when he was doing business in Wenzhou, buying fake Rolexes and returning to Guizhou to sell them where people had yet to learn that such things could be fake. The Wenzhou part of the story is what makes it so interesting. Traveling through Zhejiang and Jiangsu, he says he noticed how similar the houses were to those in his village, but he also observed that most of the old villages in that region were already "ruined" (*pohuaile*), and this convinced him that his village's old structures should be preserved. In this observation, Wang predated the local scholars by 15 years. It wasn't until the year 2000 that intellectuals began to tell villagers that they should really stop tearing down their old houses, because the houses represented a link with the past and with the prestigious world of downstream China – "China proper."

When Wang first told me this story, I was certain he was making it up. But after a number of subsequent visits, I am no longer so sure. If true, this tale either confirms his amazing ability to anticipate trends in China's reforming economy, or it simply attests to his skill in reinventing himself to suit the times. Either way, the resulting portrait is of a very intelligent and extremely savvy person. Here's another example of his ability either to anticipate the broader trends of Chinese society or at least to reinvent his history to match those trends: "Back in 1985 I was invited to speak at the No. 1 middle school [in the nearby city]. I told the students to study hard, because after the year 2000 it will be a time of knowledge competition. Their manual labor won't be needed. So if they don't study hard, they won't have a future." The reason I initially doubted his story was because of the house he himself lives in – a brash two-story and thoroughly modern cement-block house with a satellite dish on top. Villagers call it the Wang Hotel. Wang has recently put some old stone and bamboo facing on the house to make it look older, but the fact is that he built it in 1997, long after he claimed to have seen the light of preservation while buying watches in Wenzhou. Wang told me that he had wanted to recreate an ornate old-style house for his family, but was unable to because of his injuries. He couldn't work with his hands, so mangled from the fire were they.

Still, everyone else in the village says that no one even knew what preservation (*wenwu baohu*) meant until 2000. That's when the intellectuals started coming. They came mostly from the nearby city and the provincial capital. But some came from as far as Beijing – historians, linguists, sociologists, eager both to learn about this newly "discovered" subculture as well as to help guide its development by teaching villagers to recognize and value their heritage. Villagers say Wang's stories are the same ones the intellectuals started telling them in 2000. And they are right. A good example of this is Wang's readiness to claim an identity as a "Jiangnan" person, that is, someone whose ancestors came from the lower reaches of the Changjiang. Many of the Tunpu ancestors in fact did come from Jiangnan. But Wang's ancestors came from Shaanxi, a good thousand miles or so northwest of Jiangnan. His claim seems to be the result of being told by local scholars that Niuchangtun is a "Tunpu" village, and Tunpu is now promoted by the province and local government as the "living fossil" of Jiangnan culture of 600 years ago preserved on the frontier. Tunpu tourism is even marketed directly to consumers in Nanjing, with an offer to "come to Guizhou to see the lives of your ancestors!" Wang has been smart enough to see this promotion as opening the door to a new kind of cultural capital both for himself and for his village, and it's in this light that his claim of identity might be interpreted.

But I don't think Wang's claim of Jiangnan ancestry can simply be dismissed as a careful if disingenuous commercial calculation, either. By the mid-twentieth century, when Wang was born, the people who are today called Tunpu were thought to be just another kind of Miao, another kind of frontier minority. Accordingly, despite their own claim to be Han, the government labelled them Miao. So part of the Tunpu fever going on in Guizhou today involves a rehabilitation of cultural prestige, with the civilization of Jiangsu and Zhejiang as the basis for that prestige.

Still, Wang's view of Tunpu culture is nevertheless derived from what he has learned from local scholars. And while Jiangnan equals prestige to him on the one hand, Tunpu presents itself as something a bit more complicated, owing to its ancientness. Wang is clearly a progressive thinker who views the past with considerable suspicion, even as he recognizes its commercial potential. During one discussion, he was talking about the custom of "*yanzihua*," a kind of fast-paced banquet repartee said to be a hallmark of distinctive Tunpu language. He was saying that few people in Niuchangtun were masters of *yanzihua* because Niuchangtun was *kejia* and thus more civilized than other villages. This prompted me to ask if he felt Tunpu culture was therefore uncivilized. This was his response:

> In fact, this Tunpu culture is a kind of backward culture. Tunpu culture is an ancient kind of culture; it's been around a long time. Looking at it in terms of development, these people were very developed economically, had very developed knowledge. From the beginning it had very developed aspects. But in fact, this Tunpu culture...has reached back 600 years and given [history] to us; this isn't contemporary stuff, so that's why I say this, it's a kind of ancient backward culture.

So yes, it's like that. But it has also filled gaps in knowledge. It is a culture of archaeological value. It is not a contemporary advanced thing. It just provides a kind of ancient culture for investigation and research. That's how I should put it.

For Wang, Tunpu is linked specifically to the scholarly investigations which introduced the concept to him in the first place. He does not really understand it in any broad anthropological sense (that is, "culture" as a way of life), but simply as the scholarly object of "investigation and research." As such, it naturally has commercial potential, and is perhaps easily something about which claims can be made without the notion that such claims have any real bearing on one's actual sense of identity.

At any rate, Wang has virtually cornered the market on Tunpu culture in his village. And for the rest of the village, "Tunpu culture" is basically regarded as Wang's private business, his property. When officials come, or scholars, or tourists, Wang is always there to take them on his little tour, pointing out all the features of its heritage. His tour is fascinating for all its instances of making connections with Jiangnan heritage. Most of this comes from the local scholars, with whom Wang has had much contact and from whom he has learned much about Tunpu history and Tunpu culture. Wang's tour narrative lifts liberally from numerous scholarly reports that have been written about Tunpu culture. Wang has done his homework. His ability to narrate the scholarly language of "culture" with such articulation has also been instrumental in securing the continuing support of the local government, and today, because of Wang, Niuchangtun is recognized as the Tunpu village with the best relationship (*guanxi*) with the local government. This has resulted in new roads, a new school building, and decreased tuition for village children. And he has managed to stop the construction of new houses since he came back in 2000. Niuchangtun has state heritage protection status, but throughout China the regulations that such status entails are followed only to the extent local officials can enforce them. In most protected places in Guizhou, such regulations are relatively meaningless. But Wang has enforced them to the letter. In my first interview with him I asked how he had managed to do this.

"I enlist the gods for help," he said with a little twinkle in his eye and a smile on his face. "The people have all these folk superstitions, so I use these. I wrote an antithetical couplet and put it up around the village during Spring Festival. It said those who don't follow the preservation policies will be punished by the gods. People aren't afraid of me. They're afraid of the gods."

But people in Niuchangtun *are* afraid of Wang. In a neighboring village they have gone so far as to close the gates when he shows up so he can't enter the village. "He steals *our* tourists," they say. "Takes *our* revenue for himself." When I was initially interviewing other villagers in Niuchangtun, I would ask them "what is Tunpu culture?" No one could say. "*Buxiaode*!" [I don't know!] was the typical response. One even told me, "*wo bugan shuo*!" [I don't dare say]. I gradually realized that these responses were due not to a lack of understanding about this new thing called Tunpu culture—though this is a reasonable assumption, since the villagers themselves have never referred to themselves as "Tunpu," and "culture" has always simply meant going to school and learning to read, which few of them have ever done. But it became clear that they *did* know what Tunpu culture was; they just didn't want to talk to *me* about it. Tunpu culture was *Wang's* business, not theirs. And I was just another of Wang's intellectuals. They initially saw me as little more than a business consultant trying to steal their secrets for the competition. To talk about Tunpu would also be like talking about someone else's property as if it were your own. "Talk to Wang about that," they would say.

Culture was seen by the villagers as Wang's capital – they didn't dare mess with it. But like any successful business, Wang's Tunpu culture was thoroughly viewed as corrupt by almost everyone who eventually *did* talk to me. My research assistants should be credited far more than I with eventually earning the trust of the villagers. I found myself sneaking around at night with my assistants, talking to people in their houses, huddled around the stove with the dogs keeping watch. They wanted to talk, but they were afraid. It struck me as somewhat odd to be going to such lengths to talk about something as seemingly harmless as "culture." But culture was *only* understood by villagers as a regime of accumulation, rather than a way of life. And they viewed Wang's ability to dominate this regime as stemming from corruption. "How else could he have become so rich? He gives money to the officials. He owns a mine and doesn't have to pay taxes to the town. He gets the government to pay for his Tunpu culture festivals and then keeps the money for himself. We never see a cent." Some of the villagers claim that Wang isn't even really Tunpu himself, since his ancestors came from Shaanxi. "He steals Tunpu culture to make himself rich." One villager had his own ideas about Tunpu culture but wouldn't tell me what these were. He didn't want Wang to know the stories *he* had to tell about the ancestors.

In this context, my relationship with Niuchangtun remains complicated. My project is viewed by villagers as a development project rather than a study in cultural geography or heritage tourism. And rightfully so. But this means that the villagers view my presence in the village as part of the same broader set of processes that I myself have come to study. My association with Wang, of course, only reinforces that attitude. I am just another outside scholar, from whom Wang will be able to accumulate even more cultural capital. The project has thus forced me to come to terms with the goals of my relationship with Wang. While his ability to transform the abstractions of scholarship into an accumulation strategy fascinate me, I am also compelled to intervene in that process on behalf of the rest of the villagers.

Wang spends much of his time in the nearby city, drumming up business for his village and hobnobbing with officials. He goes, as the other villagers say, to *gao guanxi*, to make connections. On a recent visit to Niuchangtun, I arrived with my assistants on one of those days that Wang was gone, "making connections." So much the better, we thought. Wang's absence gave us the opportunity to meet with other villagers without having to devise strategies of avoiding him so that others could speak freely. By evening, however, Wang had gotten word that we were back in the village; he hired a mini-van and returned from the city straight away. He was waiting up for us, very agitated, when we returned to our lodgings from some late night interviewing. He had just obtained a copy of the city's tourism development plan, and he wanted to hear my suggestions for how best to succeed within the framework of the new plan. But his agitation stemmed primarily from his growing sense of frustration with the lack of unity among the villagers, and his exasperation that they regarded him as corrupt. We talked late into the night beneath a dim light bulb, huddled around the coal-stoked stove, cracking sunflower seeds. We talked about the need for openness and equality among all participants in development, and how I felt it was his responsibility more than others to foster this kind of environment for effective governance. It was our first conversation where I began to see Wang less as an obstacle to sustainable development, and more as the only viable option for implementing a feasible plan for the village's future as a tourist site. And as I write this, I maintain the hope that Wang's participation in our project will somehow yield a more democratic form of governance in the village.

What obviously fascinates me about Wang is the way he both symbolizes and embodies China's new cultural economy. He has not just benefited from the reforms. He has turned his personal narrative into a story that itself anticipated the reforms and thus is legitimized by them. And at some point, whether he is telling things the way they really occurred or inventing it all for the benefit of his many interlocutors becomes irrelevant. Either way, his ability to turn culture into capital is both astonishing to me and fortunate for his village. The provincial leaders in Guiyang could learn a lot from his shrewdness. At the same time, he offers a window into the way the reforms have enabled personal enrichment at the expense of social alienation, on the way corruption has gone hand in hand with development, and how a readjustment of attitudes toward the past and toward culture have created an entirely new regime of capital accumulation.

I hope that my relationship with Wang will result in some adjustments in his style of leadership. The project will call for several more visits to Niuchangtun and my collaborators and I are planning on holding a conference on Tunpu cultural tourism in the nearby city, as well as publishing a book in China about our research. By the time these events occur, the uncomfortable choice between interpreting a fascinating research subject and targeting for journalistic exposé another case of abusive leadership will perhaps have disappeared. I'm looking forward to telling the story about someone who has transformed himself, along with his village, and about how both have come out better for it.

Tim Oakes teaches cultural geography at the University of Colorado at Boulder. He is the author of Tourism and Modernity in China (1998) and co-editor of Travels in Paradox (2005) and Translocal China (2005).

---

[*] This material is based upon work supported by the National Science Foundation under Grant No. 0243045. The author wishes to express his thanks to Wu Xiaoping, Yang Zhu, Du Wei, Luo Yu, and Zhang Niandong for their assistance. Any opinions, findings, and conclusions or recommendations expressed in this essay are those of the author and do not necessarily reflect the views of the National Science Foundation or the author's assistants.

[1] A pseudonym.

[2] A fictitious place-name.

[3] Guizhou was one of the most enthusiastic supporters of the Great Leap Forward and one of the campaign's more radical regions of implementation. The province was promoted by Beijing as a model of the virtues of having been "poor and blank," but ultimately the Great Leap campaign reduced the province, like many throughout China, to political chaos, ethnic tensions, and famine. Between 1959 and 1965, the province lacked the ability effectively to implement any central political directives. In this environment, entrepreneurial individuals like Wang would thrive (see Yang 1996).

[4] For a political perspective on the relatively "unplanned" nature of economic reforms, see Fewsmith (1994). For similar views of the reforms from a rural perspective, see Gao (1999) and Zhou (1996).

[5] This claim is based solely on my observation of a posted list of "best-selling books in Guiyang" at the city's largest bookstore in May, 2004. *Six Hundred Years of Tunpu* was second on this list of 10 titles.

References:

Croll, E. (1994). *From Heaven to Earth: Images and Experiences of Development in China* (London: Routledge).

Fewsmith, J. (1994). *Dilemmas of Reform in China: Political Conflict and Economic Debate* (Armonk, NY: M.E. Sharpe).

Gao, M. (1999). *Gao Village: Rural Life in Modern China* (Honolulu: University of Hawaii Press).

Unger, J. and J. Xiong (1990). "Life in the Chinese hinterlands under the rural economic reforms." *Bulletin of Concerned Asian Scholars* 22(2): 4-17.

Wang, J. (2001). "Culture as leisure and culture as capital." *positions* 9(1): 69-104.

Yan D. and S. Gao. (2002). *Liubainian Tunpu – Ming Wangchao Yimin Jishi* (600 Years of *Tunpu* - A Chronicle of Ming Dynasty Folk Relics). (Guiyang: Guizhou Renmin Chubanshe).

Yang, D. (1996). *Calamity and Reform in China: State, Rural Society, and Institutional Change Since the Great Leap Famine* (Stanford: Stanford University Press).

Zhou, K. (1996). *How the Farmers Changed China* (Boulder: Westview).

The True Story of Akheu

Janet C. Sturgeon

The True Story of Akheu is of course meant to call to mind "The True Story of Ah Q",[1] although Akheu, my subject, is in many ways the opposite of Ah Q. In direct contrast to Lu Xun's Ah Q, whose insensitivity and hapless choices led ultimately to his execution, Akheu, an Akha[2] villager in Yunnan, had an astute understanding of the emerging possibilities during reform era China. For the most part he made clever choices. Like Ah Q, though, Akheu was always on the lookout for ways to get rich. In reform era China, that was a Good Thing. The last time I saw him, in 2002, Akheu was talking about a scheme to raise goats in Mengsong, his village in the autonomous prefecture of Xishuangbanna, in Yunnan province, on the ridge that separates China and Burma. In fact, he planned to organize Akha on either side of the border in a project to increase local incomes by providing goat meat to a hot pot restaurant in Shenzhen. Akheu was busy linking Akha villagers on the peripheral Southwest of China with urban and possibly international consumers in Shenzhen. How had Akheu pulled this off?

In Mengsong, Akheu came from a leading clan, [3] whose forebears had been village heads when Mengsong was part of the tiny principality of Sipsongpanna that for centuries had paid tribute to both China and Burma.[4] That cross-border relationship is important to this story. Once firmly enclosed within the People's Republic, Sipsongpanna became the Dai autonomous prefecture of Xishuangbanna. And, by changing its name to Xishuangbanna, a name without particular meaning in Chinese, the Chinese government officially erased the history of the principality, as well as China's colonial move in taking it over. In the 1950s, the Akha people in Mengsong were incorporated within the Hani minority nationality and rated at a "primitive" mode of production during ethnic identification (*minzu shibie*). During the reform era, that rating meant that Akha were considered "backward" in the realm of economic development. Akheu's relatives were heads of the Mengsong production brigade during the collective period, and later (skipping a few changes in nomenclature), heads of the administrative village[5] of Mengsong. So Akheu, the administrative village head from 1992 to 1998, was a big fish in a peripheral pond. From the outset, I viewed Akheu as charming and very smart. It was nearly impossible not to like him, even as I discovered that he was woefully corrupt. His manipulations were successful in part because other people must also have found him charismatic. This story is about how Akheu managed to connect his "out-of-the-way"[6] pond with lowland administrators in Xishuangbanna, business people in Burma, and, most recently, with a restaurant owner in Shenzhen, turning his peripheral realm into a site of possibility for his own ambitions.

The economic reform period in Mengsong entailed, as elsewhere, the dismantling of the commune in the early 1980s. In this locale, "reform" basically meant the devolution of property rights in land and trees, together with the authority to make decisions about their use, within state regulations, to households and hamlets. In this upland site, in 1982 households acquired shifting cultivation fields[7] as well as areas for wet rice, tea, bamboo, and livestock. Villagers experienced this allocation as fair and equitable, giving everyone the same shake as the reform era began. In 1984, forests were distributed to hamlets as collective forests, and to households as freehold forest for subsistence uses. In Mensong, all of these initial contracts for agricultural and forestland were for 50 years. With the gradual opening up of markets, Mengsong farmers sold cultivated products—vegetables, fruits, and livestock—and goods collected in the surrounding forests—wild fruits, medicinal herbs, bamboo, and rattan. Products that Akha farmers had used all their lives could now be sold. Farmers could compete in selling these goods in the market, leading potentially to disparity in household incomes. In common with Lei Guang's chapter in this volume, I trace the emergence of a market in Mengsong, but giving here a quite different example of how "the *actually-emerging*...market in China" is constituted by specific government policies and the practice of market agents (i.e. entrepreneurs) and government officials (Lei Guang, this volume). In this site on the periphery of China, minority nationality shifting cultivators' experience of "the market" fell under both agricultural and forest policies, as agricultural goods and non-timber forest products (NTFPs) could be sold, but timber could not. Other factors influencing market formation included the form of "development" promoted in "backward" minority nationality areas, and the central government's changing perception of forests—to be protected or used, and by whom. The configuration of "the market" in Mengsong also came to be closely tied to aspects of globalization, as China prepared for entry into the World Trade Organization (WTO).

To understand Akheu's role in the expansion of markets, we need to start earlier in his career. As a minority nationality youth in the 1970s, Akheu joined the People's Liberation Army (PLA) as an avenue for upward mobility in Mengsong and in Chinese society more broadly. The PLA made Akheu a communications officer in the area of Burma just across the border from Mengsong. He could speak Akha and some Dai, as well as Yunnanese Chinese, making him a multi-lingual border person in the service of the Chinese government. In this post Akheu developed many Burmese military and business contacts. In the PLA, Akheu joined the Chinese Communist Party and also perfected his standard Mandarin, a rare accomplishment for someone without a high school education.

When Akheu returned to Mengsong in the 1980s, he became the security officer for the administrative village. In this role he was closely linked with the township, the lowest level of state administration, and also connected with the Mengsong border military post. He maintained his contacts across the border with business people and with Burmese military and "rebel army" personnel. In this position, Akheu was well placed to take advantage of the state attention and funds funneled to this sensitive border site as markets began to play a greater role in China's development. Akheu presented himself to township and county officials as someone who was "in the know" about conditions in Burma and able to protect the border of China against the "chaos" on the other side. Through his role as border protector, as well as his delivery of goods and information from Burma to lowland administrators in Xishuangbanna, Akheu made himself into an important player well beyond the bounds of Mengsong. He then used his regional stature to become a patron in Mengsong, controlling how certain natural resources became commodities and skewing the benefits to himself, his family, and his network of cronies. Three stories illustrate Akheu's role in determining who got access to emerging resources as they became commodities in new markets: the tin story, the wasteland auction, and the lodge.

The Tin Story

When a geological survey team from Jinghong, the prefecture capital, found tin in one hamlet in Mengsong, the team hired local villagers to do the mining. Villagers initially thought the tin was being mined for some national purpose, part of a "planned economy." When they discovered that the geology team was selling the tin for its own profit, they quickly adjusted to this new possibility and wanted to mine and sell the tin themselves. This incident marked a moment of transition in villagers' understanding of a socialist market economy. Tin rapidly became a "resource" that could be bought and sold. To get rid of the geology team, villagers asked for help from Akheu, the administrative village security officer. Akheu complied with their request, but he also intervened to claim the tin as a resource belonging to the whole administrative village. According to Akheu's arrangement, anyone in Mengsong could mine the tin but then had to sell it to him for 12 *yuan* per kilo. He set up a company to collect the tin, which he sold to enterprises in Jinghong for 20 *yuan* per kilo. At that point in China (1985), any "company" had to be affiliated with a unit of government, in this case the administrative village. Under the tin agreement, Akheu was to contribute three *yuan* per kilo from the resale profits to Mengsong, the administrative village. The Mengsong accountant claimed that for the first four years, the figures never came out right. The accountant alleges that Akheu had skimmed off about 100,000 *yuan* (about US$20,000 at that time) for himself and his collaborators.

At the time of my research (1996-97), villagers in the hamlet with tin were still furious at Akheu. By the mid-1990s, tin had become the largest source of household income and villagers knew that Akheu was unfairly pocketing profits for himself. Villagers claimed that the tin was theirs and that they should be able to sell it directly to the county. They based their claim on the state property allocations of 1982 and also on their use of these lands over many generations—a customary claim. In fact, the tin belonged to the state, but the Chinese government was not concerned about who mined a small tin deposit, so long as the state received appropriate taxes when it was sold. In other words, the state was not going to protect villagers, and was more likely to support Akheu, an official at the administrative village level. In any case, Akheu got away with claiming the tin and managing a lucrative tin business because of his many connections in township government, and because of his role in securing the border through the organized mining of tin. Akheu found a way to control who could mine the tin, where the miners sold it, and who got the profits, enhancing his own role as the patron controlling resource access. State policies had made possible a market for tin that linked the village, the administrative village, the township, and the county, but in Mengsong, the market was shaped by a clever administrative village official who had connections in all of these sites.

The Wasteland Auction

In 1993, Yunnan province adopted a wasteland auction policy, allowing villages to auction degraded village lands for contracts up to 99 years to a bidder, either from the village or outside, who promised to keep the auctioned area in trees. This policy marked a change in property rights, since the auction winners were now allowed to "buy" land that had earlier been allocated to collectives. The policy was designed to increase the extent of forest cover in Yunnan and to prevent soil erosion, in line with the state's growing interest in the environment (Zuo 1997). By applying market mechanisms, the state hoped to attract entrepreneurs to invest in trees. The policy allowed the "market," in the form of auctions, to determine access to land, and also brought issues of forest management and environmental degradation into the market arena.

In Mengsong in 1995, a former hamlet head approached Akheu, by then administrative village head, about holding a wasteland auction to allow him to contract about 2000 *mu*[8] of land in the watershed of the Mengsong reservoir. Akheu and the former hamlet head signed the papers in secret to allow this former hamlet head to acquire collective land. When this man presented the papers to the township forestry station, the foresters approved the wasteland auction, since the papers stipulated that other affected villagers had all agreed to the auction. When the wasteland auction became public, however, there was a storm of protest in Mengsong. Villagers were furious, not only because the deal was done without their knowledge, but also because the auctioned area was immediately cleared and burned in preparation for planting fruit trees. A project that was supposed to prevent soil erosion was funneling silt into the reservoir, and in fact causing increased soil erosion.

Additionally, villagers worried about the accumulation of so much land in one person's hands. They claimed that they had built the reservoir with their own labor during the collective period, creating a communal resource that benefited everyone. The forest above it had been regenerating since 1970, when work on the reservoir began. In 1995, the forest was somewhat brushy, but it was sufficient to prevent erosion into the reservoir. Villagers were now nostalgic for the collective years, when, in their memory, good socialist leaders took care of everyone's needs. In their view, the accumulation of 2000 plus *mu* in one person's hands meant that this person would benefit from the auction while many others lost out. Villagers saw this as a major change in the allocation of land and a dangerous step away from the path of watching out for the whole community. They claimed that Akha custom had always been to take care of everyone in the village. While other stories suggested that, in fact, this was not always the case, the wasteland auction mobilized villagers around the narrative of Akha custom, in defense against Akheu's predations. While he may not have benefited monetarily from the auction, he increased his role as the patron of access to new resources. Villagers were concerned not just with present soil erosion, but with portents for the future. Their experience of "development" projects in the reform era had been that often a few people got rich, while many remained poor. Again, because of Akheu's connections in township administration, nurtured through the occasional delivery of wild game from Burma, the township forestry station rebuffed villagers' protests. Township officials relied on Akheu as their man on the spot, implementing state forest policies, protecting the environment, and taking care of the border. The "market" for land was of course made possible by state policy, but in this case,[9] the auction transpired in ways that benefited Akheu, reinforcing his role as the controller of resource access, and enriched one of his cronies among the local elites.

The Lodge

The third story about Akheu concerns a lodge that he built during my stay there in 1996-97. Akheu maintained that government agents needed a better place to stay in Mengsong, and that tourism was opening up for border areas. Foreign tourists would surely like to visit Akha hamlets in this glorious upland site right on the Burma border. Accordingly, Akheu organized men from his own hamlet to cut trees in the collective forest, the area designated for house construction. The men then built what looked like an oversized Akha house right along the main street. Akheu's final step was to have the lodge painted orange, green, and yellow to attract visitors. Other villagers were appalled at the lodge's appearance, saying it looked like a Han Chinese imitation of a minority nationality building, many of which they had seen in Jinghong. They feared that profits from the lodge would make their way into Akheu's personal hands. Hamlet collective labor and trees had gone into the lodge, but the benefits would flow privately to Akheu. The resource in question was not just the lodge, of course, but income from tourism, as ethnic tourism became a key selling point for Yunnan. Akheu wanted to tap into that tourist money. Other villagers judged that Akheu was using "Akha-ness" in inappropriate ways. Villagers were not opposed to tourists, nor were they averse to new money-making schemes. What they objected to was Akheu's maneuvering to benefit from the lodge at their expense. The market for tourists had been opened up by a set of provincial government policies to build a tourist industry based on Yunnan's 25 minority nationalities. Once again, the market was shaped by Akheu's maneuvering to turn collective resources into private gain. In this case, he was exploiting Akha difference from mainstream Chinese culture, using Akha marginality to market an out-of-the-way place (Tsing 1994).

There were heated complaints about Akheu's handling of these three episodes, the tin, the wasteland auction, and the lodge. The nature of the conflicts over these episodes reflects a number of trends experienced more broadly across reform era China. One way to view them is to focus on the tension in the term "socialist market economy," with some people (villagers) leaning toward the socialist side, and others (mainly Akheu) leaning toward the market economy. Villagers valued the state's involvement in the equitable distribution of resources, broad-based increases in household income, and the availability of communal resources for everyone's benefit. Akheu and his cohort valued an increasingly freewheeling market, individual competition, privately owned resources, and individual gain. These split perspectives actually represent two strands in the state's development mission. One strand encouraged household competition in growing markets to foster economic development. The other strand emphasized poverty alleviation to make rural livelihoods more secure. The two meanings of development, as market development and poverty alleviation, are also prevalent in international development thinking and are often mistakenly conflated (Ferguson 1994). Akha villagers could tell the difference, which they experienced as a contradiction.

In a general sense, villagers favored poverty alleviation, whereas Akheu favored market competition, in an arena where he could skew the market to this own private benefit. The story is not quite so simple, however, since Akha villagers *were* interested in increasing their incomes, but in a context of communal resources and general hamlet improvement—or at least, in explaining the conflict to me, that's how their argument ran, in contention with Akheu's plans. In other ways, villagers, configured as households, were competing in markets and engaged in disputes over access to lands and trees.

Villagers' most heated complaints were about what they perceived as Akheu's corrupt practices. Mengsong hamlet heads approached officials in township and county government to protest Akheu's claiming and profiting from Mengsong tin as well as conducting a secret wasteland auction. In their view, much of so-called development benefited predatory elites instead of raising everyone's income. The episode of the lodge, meanwhile, opened up a different realm of development, promoted particularly in Yunnan, to take advantage of its "cultural diversity" to attract large numbers of tourists. While this tale again illustrates Akheu exploiting collective resources for personal gain, it also shows him, in other people's estimation, catering to a Han Chinese sense of what "Akha" meant. Akheu's lively corruption in all three of these stories was also characteristic of reform era China (O'Brien and Li 1999). He was by no means the only one benefiting from the devolution of property rights and responsibilities to the local level, a process that allowed many local elites to enrich themselves at other people's expense.[10]

In 1998, Akheu's fortunes changed. He had done well in the reform era, but the good times were coming to an end. By 1998 his corrupt practices had either gone too far or become too blatant. Akheu had bought a new truck in Burma to avoid paying the 100 percent duty on new cars in China. For many weeks he drove around Mengsong and down as far as the township with Burmese license plates on his truck. Akheu approached township officials about getting him Chinese plates, sweetening his request with the carcass of a barking deer from Burma. Without the Chinese plates, he couldn't drive to Jinghong to take his two children back to school. When Akheu and his children returned to Mengsong with the Burmese plates still on, it was clear that a barking deer had not done the trick. Within a few months, township officials removed from office Akheu and two others in the administrative village. It was bruited about that financial improprieties had gotten them into trouble. Since corruption was common in the township and in Jinghong, it's possible that Akheu just hadn't bribed the right person, or hadn't contributed enough. Villagers, of course, thought that their persistent complaints had brought him down. Once out of office, Akheu and his wife moved to Baoshan, a town in western Yunnan, where he had a three-year contract to run a tin mine. According to his wife, they invested 100,000 yuan in the tin mine, and lost it all. In late 2001, Akheu returned to Mengsong in failure.

In the period between 1998, when Akheu left for Baoshan, and his return in late 2001, a series of important events occurred in China. Deng Xiaoping died in 1997, ushering in an era of rethinking and reshuffling among top leaders in

Beijing. They were preparing for 2002, when new national leadership would be chosen. Among their considerations were China's possible entry into the World Trade Organization (WTO), and the growing disparities in income between the country's eastern and western regions (Goodman 2004, 2001). Debates centered on how to prepare China for WTO, and how both to alleviate poverty in the West and to integrate the West more firmly within China (Goodman 2004, 2001; Economy 2002). There was also discussion of how to reduce the corruption at county and township levels, especially in Western China (O'Brien and Li 1999).

In 1998 massive floods along the Yangtze River and in Heilongjiang in the northeast killed hundreds of people and caused massive damage. Central leaders interpreted these floods as national environmental disasters, caused in part, it was claimed, by deforestation along the upper watersheds of the Yangtze. In response, the government instituted a logging ban that gradually extended across western China. The logging ban meant that the state was now reclaiming responsibility for those forests allocated to villages and households in the early reform era. The overreach of the policy is shown by the fact that the logging ban eventually included Mengsong, even though Mengsong is actually located in the Mekong River watershed. Additionally, my forest measurements from 1997 had shown Mengsong forests to be in good condition. The "cut of one knife" logging ban policy, though, was implemented across Western China without reference to local conditions.

In 2000, central leaders launched the Open Up the West, or Go West project (*xibu dakaifa*), one of several regional projects to improve China's infrastructure and technology in preparation for the foreign investment that, it was presumed, would flood in as a result of China's accession into WTO (Goodman 2001). One component of Go West was called "ecological construction," a campaign to mobilize farmers across the West to re-green the landscape. Forestry departments paid villagers to plant trees in any "wastelands" with a slope of 25 degrees or greater, and farmers were enjoined either to let trees regenerate or to plant trees on sloping agricultural fields (Economy 2002). Through a policy called "grain for green," farmers were to receive 150 kilos of grain and 20 *yuan* per year for eight years for each *mu* of cultivated land that regenerated into trees. The scale of labor mobilization to accomplish reforestation was reminiscent of Maoist campaigns, but here the labor was organized to prepare China's environment for the international standard represented by WTO (Jhaveri 2003). Ecological construction was a further step in the state's reclaiming land and trees and even extending the area of forest under forestry department control. In line with notions prevalent in international environmental projects, the meaning of forests also changed, from being subsistence resources allocated to farmers, to being environmental resources protected by the state.

In March 2002, during my visit, Jiang Zemin and Zhu Rongji were on television every night as they visited cities across Western China. They were explaining the reasons for the inclusion of business people (in addition to peasants and workers) in the ranks of citizens represented by the Chinese Communist Party (CCP). Business people would be in a starring role in the international capitalist economy, signified by the WTO, which China was very pleased to join.

This series of somewhat disparate events represents changes that combined to produce devastating outcomes in Mengsong. The reform era from 1982 to 1997 entailed the devolution of property rights and decision-making to the local level in rural areas in a bid to increase agricultural productivity (Goodman 2004). From 1998 onward, the state re-centralized authority over forests, and re-inserted itself in large-scale plans for the West and preparation for WTO. While the meaning and outcome of these broad-scale changes, especially Go West, remain anything but clear (see Goodman 2004), the results for forest-dependent villagers are more apparent, and more ominous.

By the time Akheu returned to Mengsong in October 2001, several changes had already taken place. The logging ban and ecological construction were in place, meaning that the forestry department had reclaimed the collective forest and household freehold forests as belonging to the state. Additionally, under ecological construction, the forestry department required Akha farmers to plant either pine trees or tea on their pasturelands. With the loss of pasture, farmers had sold off almost all their livestock, formerly a major source of household income. At the same time, the logging ban prevented farmers from cutting trees larger than a certain girth on their shifting cultivation lands. Without cutting the trees, farmers couldn't get a good burn. As a result, most shifting cultivation lands were regenerating into forests, meaning that the forestry department would reclaim these lands, too. The state had not only taken back the forest, but also extended its area onto what had been farmers' fields and pastures. The logging ban and ecological construction in tandem had wrought a major dispossession in Mengsong. The loss ensued from a government judgment that upland farmers, especially minority nationality ones, were partly responsible for the deforestation that had caused the 1998 floods. "Backward" minorities were being removed from resources that they didn't know how to "manage."

Another change in Mengsong was that all mining of tin and other minerals was now contracted out to firms from Fujian, Guangdong, and Kunming. These companies hired laborers from elsewhere to do the mining. The firms paid a fee to Mengsong, but that didn't contribute to household incomes. Contracting arrangements that in urban areas could foster creative marketing arrangements (see Lei Guang, this volume) in this upland rural area managed to deprive local farmers of the benefit from minerals found on their lands.

As a result of both ecological construction and the loss of income from mining, household incomes in Mengsong dropped by 25 percent between 1997 and 2002. In February 2002, Mengsong was officially declared a "poor village." The rise in prominence of business people, in this case the mining contractors, had impoverished Mengsong villagers. The minerals in Mengsong and the profits from their sale now flowed away from Mengsong. The state's reclaiming the forest meant that villagers lost much of their pasture, agricultural land, and forests to the official forestry department. The staples of their economic life—herding, forestry, mining, and agriculture—were denied them.

In this new context, Akheu was remaking himself, step by step, into an entrepreneur. Instead of being an ethnic minority farmer, one of those "backward" people who destroyed the environment, he would become a forward-thinking entrepreneur who contributed to China's economic growth. He was no longer pursuing state office, but was instead becoming a regionally important person through another avenue, as a businessperson valued by the CCP. Through his experience in tin mining (however uneven), Akheu knew provincial mining contractors, and convinced one of them to hire him. Akheu was now the head of the tin contract in Mengsong, mediating between the firm in Kunming and the team of outside workers hired to dig out the tin. Additionally, Akheu was the point person for the transport of a special kind of rattan from Yeren Shan in Burma to a furniture factory in Kunming. While in Mengsong, the rattan was stored in the colorful lodge, which had never attracted many visitors. Local people claimed that a ghost lived in the lodge—they were unwilling even to hold meetings there. But the lodge served well as a warehouse for rattan.

The most creative idea, however, was the goat project. Akheu was busy organizing Akha in Burma and Mengsong to raise goats. In a new guise, he constituted himself as an important border mediator and patron of a new business. He was setting out to organize and control the border in a new way. Perhaps most tellingly, Akheu devised this new project in the face of adversity. In January 2002, his daughter had been killed in a truck accident in which the driver, the Han Chinese husband of the Mengsong doctor, also lost his life. At the Mengsong memorial service for the doctor's husband, one of the deceased's relatives from Shenzhen got into conversation with Akheu. As the convergence of interests became apparent, the goat raising scheme was developed, right on the spot. The Shenzhen relative owned a hot pot restaurant, but had a hard time getting a reliable supply of goat meat. Akheu quickly responded that a mountain environment was ideal for raising goats, and that Mengsong Akha could use a new moneymaking venture. Following the memorial service, Akheu visited his elder sister, an expert in the agriculture office in Jinghong. She was ready with services and possible funding to help with the goat scheme. Akheu planned to apply to the Go West project for additional funding—the only person in Mengsong who mentioned Go West. Akheu was ready to serve as one of the entrepreneurs that the CCP was highlighting as critical to China's future. He had hooked up with possibilities created by China's globalization from his position on the far periphery, making good use of his out-of-the-way place.

A reprise of the themes covered here relate to the market, the state, and China's moves toward globablization with respect to Akha upland villagers and our hero, Akheu. The reform era was characterized, in Mengsong and elsewhere, by a so-called "socialist market economy," a term replete with somewhat contradictory impulses. The two strands within the state's development mission, to foster a market economy on a competitive basis, and to alleviate poverty, signify the disparities involved. There were state initiatives for the equitable distribution of resources, such as land allocations to households and collectives. There were also state programs for poverty alleviation, particularly in Western China. On the other hand, the state opened up markets and encouraged increasing market competition over a growing number of goods. Villagers configured as households were to manage their own affairs in competition with others. The devolution of responsibility for local management, in addition to other factors not mentioned here, allowed for considerable corruption at local levels of government as well as in administrative villages. Indeed, widespread corruption was a hallmark of the reform era, one that central leaders wanted to address.

Following the 1998 floods, the central government imposed a logging ban that eventually embraced most of Western China and re-instituted state responsibility for and management of forestlands. As China geared up for WTO, business people rose in importance, underscored by their inclusion among those represented by the CCP. Under projects such as Go West, the central government promoted grand schemes, envisioning the West as a receptacle for massive investment. There was a heady feeling of political mobilization about the Go West plans, even though the context was preparation for full entry into an international capitalist economy. While Go West may fail to reach most of its stated goals, since state investment has been limited and foreign investment not particularly forthcoming (Goodman 2004), the ecological component of it, in conjunction with the logging ban, may have the most enduring long term effects.

For Akha villagers in Mengsong, the events of recent years have entailed a loss of land, forests, and livestock—those resources equitably allocated to them in 1982-84. Villagers have also experienced a loss of income from mining. Their plummeting incomes qualified Mengsong as a "poor village" by 2002. From their perspective, recent years ushered in a massive dispossession of their resources, and the benefits of the reform era were gone. Their minority ethnicity, peripheral locale, and ostensible backwardness had played into these losses, all brought about by state plans.

Akheu, on the other hand, had remade himself once again. He read well the signs of where China was heading and who would be winners and losers as China entered WTO. In realms of entrepreneurship, his minority ethnicity was less important than his experience and skills, or stated differently, his minority ethnicity might play out to his advantage as a result of his experience and skills. Akheu contracted to mine in Mengsong, and organized people into a new business venture in raising goats. He connected with a restaurant in Shenzhen, giving him links to a cosmopolitan urban area. He inserted Mengsong into the rattan trade between Burma and China. He managed to use his border locale once again to enhance his position and turn a peripheral site into a node of business and exchange with Burma and elsewhere in China. Like Ah Q of Lu Xun's tale, he was always looking to get rich and suffered ups and downs in his quest. But unlike Ah Q, he was able again and again to join a going concern—the PLA, administrative village government, and now business ventures—at the right time. Akheu was clever and charismatic, persuasive and enthusiastic. I had to stop myself from investing in the goat project, remembering just in time that I would lose my shirt. Unlike other Mengsong villagers, who had lost out in a major way under new forest policies and preparations for WTO, Akheu had set himself up to go with the upward flow. He had astutely read and helped shape the "actually-emerging market" constituted by government policies, state agents, and entrepreneurs. As an ethnic minority person on the periphery of China, Akheu had been surprisingly successful at using his marginal locality to help mold the market to suit his own plans.

Janet C. Sturgeon is Assistant Professor in the Geography Department, Simon Fraser University. She is the author of *Border Landscapes: The Politics of Akha Land Use in China and Thailand* (2005).

---

[1] For the original story, see *The Complete Stories of Lu Xun.*

[2] Akha are subsumed within the official Hani minority nationality in China. Since they call themselves Akha, that is the name used here.

[3] Unless otherwise cited, data are from fieldwork from November 1995 to March 1997, and from follow up visits in March and July 2002.

[4] See Giersch 1998 for a history of Sipsongpanna as a "buffer" between China and Burma.

[5] The names have been changed again. Mengsong is now a "village" (*cun*) and hamlets have become "small groups" (*xiaozu*). To avoid confusion I use the terms from 1997.

[6] This refers to Anna Tsing's *In the Realm of the Diamond Queen*), an examination of marginality in an "out of the way" place, in which "shifting cultivators. . .worked to define and re-define their situation on the periphery of state power" (p. 5).

[7] Shifting cultivators cut upland forest to open fields, burn the slash to fertilize the soil, plant grain for a year or two, and then fallow the site for 13 to 15 years (in this area) to allow trees to regenerate.

[8] 15 *mu* equals one hectare.

[9] For an extended discussion of the conflicts and corruption involved in wasteland auctions in Sichuan, see Grinspoon 2002.

[10] In our recent article (Sturgeon and Sikor 2004), Thomas Sikor and I explored the dynamics of postsocialist property rights in rural resources in Bulgaria, Albania, Vietnam, and China. We found that in postsocialist contexts, local elites were invariably the winners in claiming resources or in the process of their allocation.

References:

Economy, Elizabeth. 2002. "China's Go West Campaign: Ecological Construction or Ecological Exploitation?" *China Environment Series*, Issue 5. Environmental Change and Security Project, Woodrow Wilson Center.

Ferguson, James. 1994. *The Anti-Politics Machine: "Development," Depoliticization, and Bureaucratic Power in Lesotho*. Minneapolis: University of Minnesota Press.

Giersch, C. Patterson 1998. "Qing China's Reluctant Subjects: Indigenous Communities and Empire Along the Yunnan Frontier." Ph.D. dissertation, Yale University.

Goodman, David S.G. 2004. "The Campaign to 'Open Up the West': National, Provincial-level and Local Perspectives," *China Quarterly*:317-334.

Goodman, David S.G. 2001. "The Politics of the West: equality, nation-building and colonization." Institute for International Studies, University of Technology, Sydney.

Grinspoon, Elisabeth. 2002. "Socialist Wasteland Auctions: Privatizing Collective ForestLand in China's Economic Transition." PhD dissertation, University of California, Berkeley.

Jhaveri, Nayna. "Ecological Construction, China's 'Go West' Campaign and Globalization," Presentation at American Association of Geographers Meetings, New Orleans, LA, March 5-9, 2003.

Lu Xun, *The Complete Stories of Lu Xun*, 1981. Translated by Yang Xianyi and Gladys Yang. Bloomington: Indiana University Press; Beijing: Foreign Languages Press.

O'Brien, Kevin and Lianjiang Li. 1999. "Selective Policy Implementation in Rural China," *Comparative Politics* 32(2):167-186.

Polanyi, Karl. 1957. "The Economy as Instituted Process," in C. Arensburg and H. Pearson, eds, *Trade and Market in the Early Empire*. Glencoe, IL: The Free Press.

Sturgeon, Janet C. and Thomas Sikor. 2004. "Post-socialist property in Asia and Europe: Variations on 'Fuzziness,'" *Conservation and Society* 2(1):1-17.

Sturgeon, Janet C. 2005. *Border Landscapes: the Politics of Akha Land Use in China and Thailand.* Seattle: University of Washington Press.

Tsing, Anna. 1993. *In the Realm of the Diamond Queen: Marginality in an Out-of the Way Place*. New Jersey: Princeton University Press.

Zuo Ting. "Institutional Constraints of Social Forestry Development in Yunnan, China." Presentation at the Regional Center on Forestry (RECOFT) Seminar, Community Forestry at the Crossroads: Reflections and Future Directions in the Development of Community Forestry, Bangkok, July 1997.

Through The Social Jungle: Mrs. Zhang And Work

Jean-Louis Rocca

Born in 1955 in Beijing, Mrs. Zhang has always remained attached to her peasant origins. Her parents left the district of Changping, near Beijing, to become workers in a new machinery company created at the beginning of the 1950s. A few months later, she was born in the village where one of her grandparents is still living. From these origins, she has retained her local *(tu)* accent and her open manners. She returns to her native village now two or three times a year to see an uncle, her aunt and some cousins.

She attended primary and secondary school in a neighborhood quite close to the work unit *(danwei)* where her parents worked. The company provided them a flat. From that period she has kept a taste for collective activities: "We were accustomed to living in a community with my parents' fellow-workers and neighbors. There were no differences among us, no envy. There was much less pressure and tension than there is nowadays. The only concern was the political campaigns. But otherwise life flowed along peacefully."

The first years of the reforms

As a result of the Cultural Revolution, Mrs.. Zhang discontinued her studies after her the second year of junior high school *(chuzhong)*. For two years she was "waiting for employment" *(daiye)*, and then in 1973 she started to work in the company of her uncle—a public transportation firm—as an office worker. Over time, she advanced through the career grades little by little to attain the level of assistant director of social welfare *(fuli)*. She was married in 1982 to a worker in a building firm and gave birth to a daughter in 1984. For her, the 1980s did not bring much change. Her company began to implement "new management methods" but this did not cause much disruption. In fact, the biggest change affected the work of the drivers, especially in the rationalization of their routes and working hours. In the offices, the only changes were those affecting accounting and the initiation of training sessions on the "modern management of the firm."

The biggest change came when Mrs. Zhang's brother-in-law "took the plunge" *(xiahai)* to create his own business. Mrs. Zhang had introduced a colleague to her sister some years before, and the two couples became very close. In 1987, Mr. Liu, the brother-in-law, decided to create his own private *(geti)* transportation firm by buying one vehicule, and then another from his former firm's trucks. He did not resign officially from his firm but was placed on extended leave: "Doing this, he took less risk. At the time, we didn't know what was going to happen, whether or not private enterprises would be allowed to continue for a long time. I nearly opened my own shop at the time. It was next to the Temple of Heaven. But my husband didn't want me to. He was afraid that neighbors would look at us in a strange way, that we would become 'different.' He was also afraid that we would have problems if official policies changed." Nonetheless, Mrs. Zhang's husband helped out his brother-in-law occasionally by cleaning or repairing vehicles. When he helped him, Mr. Liu compensated him.

At first, the democracy demonstrations in Beijing of 1989 were witnessed with a lot of excitement. "Such events had never before been seen in Beijing. We participated in two marches with our firm, but gradually the excitement declined. We began to be afraid and stayed at home. Later, there were meetings in the neighborhoods and in workplaces. We were asked if we knew of people sought by the authorities or of students who had stayed on Tiananmen Square until the end. But in our firm, no one was denounced. The officials didn't press the point, perhaps because they themselves had been on the Square. We listened to speeches and studied official texts, and then things went along as before. The only problem was that my brother-in-law abandoned his transport firm and returned to his original enterprise. Until 1991, one was better off not being too interested in private commerce. But he did leave the trucks in the garage."

Things began to move again in 1991. Free markets reopened. But Mr. Liu waited until 1993 to start up his activity again, once the reforms had been re-launched in 1992. In the end he left his original firm in 1996 when the company began to put employees into the category of *xiagang* (laid off).[1] He sold his firm and then came into contact with a foreign transportation company, and signed up with the company, being placed in charge of teams of movers.

Disruption at the end of the 1990s

For Mrs. Zhang, however, things got worse in the 1990s. From 1994 on, rumors spread about the restructuring of state firms, and in 1996 the first *xiagang zhigong* (laid-off staff and workers) were given notice. At the beginning, the measure was called temporary, but in 1998 a reemployment service center (*zaijiuye fuwu zhongxin*) was opened in the firm and the "victims" were openly told that they had to find a new employer within three years. "The oldest were the first to be put on *xiagang* status. But the trend did not stop there. New names were continually announced. I was dismissed in 1997. People were not happy at all, but no one supported us. On the contrary, the unions explained that it was for China's development and for a future improvement in living standards. Nearly the entire office of the social welfare office disappeared."

The *xiagang zhigong* received a modest compensation, 400 *yuan* per month, compared to a previous monthly wage of 1,050 *yuan*. Fortunately for Mrs. Zhang, the firm continued to give her free medical care. The transportation sector, it should be mentioned, was able to fulfil the requirements of "market forces" without too much difficulty. After 1999, Mrs. Zhang's firm became essentially profitable. But at the same time, personnel rolls have dropped from more than 2,000 workers to fewer than 1,000.

Mr. Zhang, in turn, became *xiagang zhigong* in 1998. The shock was great to him and he has never since found true employment. He received training to become a taxi driver, but he became ill and has not worked regularly ever since. He does part-time work, sometimes at the request of his residents' committee or his friends. His pay "doesn't exceed a few hundred *yuan* each month at the most." In 2001, having used up the three years allowable in *xiagang zhigong* status, he was no longer eligible for social benefits and no longer received a stipend. But he refused to enroll as unemployed while the family revenues just barely exceeded the poverty level.[2] Mrs. Zhang took advantage of the situation by requesting early retirement which, with an income of 900 *yuan*, is much more advantageous for her. It appears that the husband's firm did not have the right to put Mr. Zhang into the *xiagang* category, since Mrs. Zhang had already met the same fate.[3] But apparently the firm wanted to get rid of Mr. Zhang.

As a result of these events, the family revenue dropped from 2000 *yuan* per month to 1300—plus the revenue coming from the "petty jobs" of Mr. Zhang—just when new expenses were needed. First, Mrs. Zhang's daughter started her higher education studies, albeit in a small university, the University of Hebei, but the expenses were nonetheless considerable. Then the brother of Mrs. Zhang began to show the first signs of an incurable disease, which turned out to be multiple sclerosis. The treatment was entirely covered by the health insurance fund but "comfort" drugs, such as analgesics, were at the family's expense.

Finally, Mrs. Zhang's sister was also placed in early retirement and her monthly income came to no more than 700 *yuan*. She was a school teacher and lost her job because of a considerable decline in the number of students, after which her school was combined with another. "We had two tough years. Fortunately, my brother-in-law found work in a foreign company. Thanks to his salary of 3500-4000 *yuan* per month we've been able to survive. When we lacked money he helped us out, but this couldn't last indefinitely. My situation didn't really change, especially regarding my husband, who became more and more sullen."

In the market economy

The solution came from the school-teacher sister. One of her colleagues, who also had been placed in early retirement, was hired as an *ayi* (babysitter) by a school attended by foreigners' children. Thanks to this colleague, Mrs. Zhang's sister came into contact with a family of Americans working for an international organization, and she was hired to take care of the couple's three children. She does not do any housework or cooking, chores which are handled by a young migrant from Anhui province.[4] Mrs. Zhang's sister is only responsible for the children's education. The parents hired her because of her teaching experience: "As I have been trained as a teacher, the parents have confidence in me. They know that I am not going to put the children in front of the TV set. I make them play, I teach them nursery rhymes and songs." The beginning was difficult because of the obstacles created by the management of the building where the expatriate family lived. It is a residence reserved for diplomats, and the service staff working for families living there must normally be hired by a firm in charge of managing service workers for foreigners. The host family had to negotiate so that Mrs. Zhang's sister could be hired without being a salaried employee of the management firm, which would have entailed a substantial portion of her salary being retained by that firm. Finally, due to her "early retirement" status, to her origins as a Beijing native, and to her expertise, Mrs. Zhang's sister was able to become an employee of the family. She receives 2000 *yuan* per month but no benefits other than the limited amount she gets as an early retiree.

In time, Mrs. Zhang was recommended by her sister to other foreign families known to the first family. She too has experienced problems with building management firms. But Mrs. Zhang is the pushy type, typical of the *laopo* (literally, wife, but also used to describe a very assertive woman) of the capital city. She is not easily taken advantage of and can argue for hours if necessary, insisting on her problems. She explains also that she is a true Beijing native, honest and hard-working, and that with her there will be no problems of theft or misdeeds the way there could be with migrants. Worn down, her antagonists generally give in and issue her the necessary work permit. Thanks to her sociability, she then succeeds in winning over the building managers. On just one occasion she had to give a small bribe.

At present, Mrs. Zhang works for three families, one from Singapore, one French, and one American. She tends to the children but also does housework and cooks. "I like my work a lot. During the two years I stayed at home, I was really depressed. I spent the entire day with my husband, who kept moaning over the past and against the reforms. I thought I would go mad. Now I see people and above all people who are very different. All day long, I am away from my home and my husband. I learn a lot of things about others. It isn't easy because the children of foreigners are very different from ours: they are more resourceful, more independent. But I like them a lot, especially the smallest ones. Often the parents don't have time to pay attention to them because foreigners have a lot of children. As a result, the children are very affectionate with me. The bosses are generally kind, they pay well and don't cause problems. The least rich are the most generous. It's like in China: when you earn a lot of money you become stingy."

Today Mrs. Zhang earns more than 2500 *yuan* per month in addition to her pension. She can therefore pay without difficulty for the schooling of her daughter and save money for her daughter to study abroad. "Today, you have to study abroad to have a good job. My goal is of course to live better. I would like to buy a car because I live far from where the foreigners live and at night I am afraid to come back home cycling. But the most important thing is my daughter and her future." Despite her departure from her old firm, Mrs. Zhang remains tied to her *danwei*. She has a cell phone paid for by her former employer. She also goes on pleasure trips organized by her old co-workers. One should point out that the firm, which has made substantial profits, has begun to provide its employees with better social protection. It has created a supplementary health insurance program and resumed its social activities. Mrs. Zhang, who remains in touch with her former bosses, takes advantage of these programs as a retiree of the *danwei*.

In 2003, however, a new misfortune befell Mrs. Zhang. She was told that her residential building would be pulled down to make way for a park. At first, opposition was very intense. Most of the residents had encountered the same job difficulties as Mrs. Zhang. They were able to keep going only because of their low-cost housing. Mrs. Zhang currently pays 200 *yuan* per month, while for the same sized apartment (around forty square meters) in the new buildings of the neighborhood, she would have to spend 3,000 to 4,000 *yuan*. Discussions are underway. "Of course we are offered financial assistance to buy an apartment elsewhere, but with the proposed amount of help the only housing we could find now would be in the area of the fifth ring road, far away from the center of town. How do they expect me to go to work from there? Way out there, there is no bus and it is too far to come in by cycling. It could work if I had a car but there are more and more traffic jams. Besides, my husband would not agree to leave this neighborhood and the few friends that he has left. We would have more room but what's the point when you are always away from home? Here, we have our routine, we know where to go to get treated or to buy some vegetables." For now, negotiations continue. The street office organized a meeting where the changes were justified in terms of the good of the country. The residents were told that renovation is a matter of beautification for the Olympic Games, but is also to render the area more pleasant for city-dwellers. "We were told that Peking lacked green areas and that the city should be modernizing according to this plan. We agree, but on condition that we are not displaced just anywhere."

Contingency and structure in the life of Mrs. Zhang

From Mrs. Zhang's life since the reforms, one can draw several conclusions. The first one is the rapidity of change. The situation of individuals has been in constant flux and everyone must adapt very quickly. This capacity to adapt is variable from one person to the other. Similarly, one must take into account the factor of chance. That Mrs. Zhang's sister is a teacher and that one of her colleagues works in a school for children of foreigners illustrates the point. Nonetheless, the role of social organizations is also determining. At each step, it is Mrs. Zhang's network of relations and her status—as a needy Beijing native—on which she relies. Personal relations (*guanxi)* indeed constitute "trust areas" that tend to become institutionalized and that determine as such the behavior and the power of the individual.[5] Opportunities and personal aptitude for adaptation have their effects within an ordered world.[6] If Mrs. Zhang's sister was able to take advantage of her relations with a former colleague, it is because she possessed a certain social status. From this perspective, the maintenance of an urban identity, defined in distinction to the social group of rural migrants in the city, is an important factor. City-dwellers, even *xiagang zhigong*, are able to retain their old status as "upstanding" folk.

The importance of overlapping connections between different social spheres must also be stressed. Mrs. Zhang has an official income (her pension) and an unofficial income (from her work in the families of foreigners). She sustains her connections with her former firm and imagines that these ties could be useful in finding work for her daughter. Her brother-in-law took the risk of entering the private sector but his wife did not—until she was compelled to. But this phenomenon is not just the result of chance or of the superior abilities of some individuals. It is also the result of "policies," even if these have not been officially adopted. For example, the brother-in-law was able to create his own company without leaving his *danwei*, and Mrs. Zhang was able to keep her apartment. We see here, in actual social interactions at the most basic level, the incrementalism of reforms that could otherwise be extremely violent.[7]

Finally, one must insist on the sometimes contradictory nature of reforms. For example, the return of a kind of "welfare system," benefiting in particular the employees of public enterprises or agencies, reveals the paradoxes of a political orientation that otherwise inclines toward favoring strict "economic rationality."[8]

Jean-Louis Rocca is a Research Fellow, Centre d'études et de recherches internationals, Fondation nationale des sciences politiques, Paris.

---

[1] This statute provides a kind of screen between work and unemployment for those dismissed who do not find another job. The employee no longer works for the firm but retains a connection: s/he receives a stipend, enjoys retraining benefits and is given job offers.

[2] China has a system of social insurance assuring a vital minimum for urban residents (*zhongguo chengshi jumin zuidi shenghuo baozhangxian zhidu)[*known too as the *zuidi shenghuo baozhang*, or minimum livelihood guarantee (ed.)]. When family income goes below a certain level—which varies according to the living standards of the city--a living subsidy must be granted.

[3] There are in many cities' regulations, more often honored in the breach than in reality, stating that it is not permitted to lay off one spouse in families where the other spouse has already been laid off.

[4] In Beijing, cleaning ladies and nannies traditionally come from this province. See Davin.

[5] See Eisenstadt Roniger.

[6] On these matters see Norbert.

[7] On this point see Rocca.

[8] See Liu and Niu.

References :

Davin, Delia. 2003. "Country Maids in the City: Domestic Service as an Agent of Modernity in China," In Françoise Mengin and Jean-Louis Rocca (eds), *Politics in China: Moving Frontiers.* London and New York: Palgrave, pp. 143-56.

Eisenstadt S. Noah and Luis Roniger. 1984. *Patrons, Clients and Friends. Interpersonal Relations and the Structure of Trust in Society.* Cambridge: Cambridge University Press.

Liu Jian and Niu Xiaohan. 2002. "Accès à la propriété et formation d'une classe moyenne à Pékin" *Perspectives chinoises,* 74 (Novembre-Decembre), pp. 4-20.

Norbert, Elias. 1991. *The Society of Individuals* .Oxford: Basil Blackwell.

Rocca, Jean-Louis. 2003. "The Rise of the Social and the Chinese State," *China Information,* XVII, 1, pp. 1-27.

The Life of a Former State Worker

Antoine Kernen

Zhou Xiwu, a jovial 50-year-old man, lives with his wife in a clean and tiny flat on the fifth floor of a newly built residential building. On the wall next to the entrance hang two photographs of the family, one in Dongying's flourishing park, the other taken during the wintertime in Harbin's Stalin Park. Mr. Zhou used to work as a specialised worker in a state-owned entreprise (SOE), making mainly metal products. His enterprise went bankrupt in 1998. This event propelled the family into several difficult years. Four years before we met, he found a new job in a Taiwanese company. Now, he has become more confident about his future in the newly built city of Dongying in Shandong Province. When talking about the past, Zhou Xiwu was full of mixed feelings. The story that follows is his.

My childhood in the countryside

Although I spent most of my life as a worker, I was born, on the 29th of December 1954, into a peasant family in Northeast China, the youngest child in the family. I have three elder sisters and one elder brother. Before I was 18, I used to live with my family in the village of Yongsheng, which is situated in Gulong county, about 400 kilometres southeast of Harbin, not far from Inner Mongolia. Formerly a Manchu village, the farmers there relied on cattle breeding, mostly horses and sheep. At the beginning of the last century, my grandparents, together with hundreds of poor peasant families from different villages in Shandong, migrated to Manchuria. This part of the Chinese empire was at that time much less populated and my family hoped to have a better life there. This migration was encouraged by the central government in order to respond to the Russian imperialistic pressure on Manchuria. As the land was administratively distributed to the migrant families near the existing railway, my village was not very far from the station of Xinzhan. Even if this migration was partly organized, my parents, who still remember some Manchu words, used to talk about the friction with the Manchu families, who were progressively pressed to move and to cede their land to new Chinese migrants. Yongsheng was, when I was born, already a Chinese village of about 300 families cultivating corn, sorghum, and soybeans.

After the Revolution, despite having very little land, my family was classified as "lower-middle peasant" (*xiazhongnong*). Their designation by this label was probably the result of the work they once had done for one of the richest peasants of the village who owned some land. My father worked for him on a contractual basis, with the license to hire additional labourers for him as need arose. As this petty landlord left the village a few months before the communists arrived there, leaving behind the tools and horses we had leased from him, we had more tools than the average peasant did. My mother used to recall that period as the golden time of her life. She enjoyed reminding us of the lively meals during harvest time, when the men working in the fields came to our place to eat what the women had cooked. This status of tenant peasant saved us from undergoing the government's investigations. Things turned out very differently for those classified as "landlords" or "rich peasants," a group amounting to about 20 percent of the village's population whose members were heavily persecuted. Under the Communists, my family was incorporated into a work group comprised of about ten families, of which my father served as the chief. My family endured the normally rough life of peasants in a poor Northeast village, but we could still manage to have enough to feed ourselves.

As had my older brother and sisters before me, I started school at the age of eight to complete the nine-year compulsory education program, graduating at the age of 17. At that time, primary education was free of charge and almost all of the village's children went to school. In the worst case, children finished only their primary school studies. My older brother participated in the same program that I did. In my family, two of my elder sisters were particularly successful in their studies. Surely they were clever and very hard working, but also at that time, our village school and the county college had some very highly motivated and well-trained teachers. My eldest sister, Zhou Yaqin, was admitted into the Harbin Nursing School in 1955 after primary school in our village and junior high school at the Gulong County. The second sister, Zhou Yarong, even got into Heilongjiang University in Harbin after three more years of study at the Zhaoyuan district's high school. Later she became professor in the Medical University of Harbin. She married a young English professor and had three daughters. She still lives in Harbin today. But after their time, the village did not see any of its pupils leaving the village for university. So the whole family and even the whole village are proud of my second sister. As a young person, I admired my elder sisters' successes, but I myself failed to proceed with higher education. Besides attending to school, like other children of my age, I used to help my family doing farm work. My childhood was thus very similar to any boy in the remote and poor countryside. Later on in my life, I benefited from the experience of living a hard life in the countryside.

The Cultural Revolution did not have much impact on the village, probably for the simple reason that the road from Gulong wasn't good at all and the nearest train station was quite far away. We lived a bit outside of this mass movement and in fact in general did not experience much in the way of campaigns or mass events. Only once, a group of Red Guards arriving from

Gulong County disturbed our usual life in the village. For some reason I forget today, they criticized and brutalized our village teachers in a public meeting. The older teacher tried to calm down the Red Guards, but his reaction excited them even more; the outcome was that our schoolteacher was beaten to death. After that, nobody in the village dared react to or tried to kick the Red Guards out, but they left a few days later and we returned to our usual life.

I move to the city

In 1972, I had an opportunity to leave the village for the small city of Suihua. I was surely very motivated to find my way out of the village, as my elder brother was assigned to remain at home to take care of my parents and land. I felt very lucky since very few children from the countryside were able to leave their home villages at that time. But this migration would never have been possible without my older sister. When she was studying in Harbin, she met another student, called Wang Shougui, from the harbour of Yingkou in Liaoning Province, who was studying in a technical institute in Wanggang District. After graduation, they married. My sister was appointed doctor at the District Hospital of Gulong, and placed in charge of the general medicine section, even though her specialty was gynecology. Her husband joined her some time later, after having landed a job as an engineer at the Gulong tractor center, and they remained in Gulong for more than ten years. Very often, the couple came to visit us. My brother-in-law, who had a good temper and often helped us in the field, was very well accepted by our family. As an "engineer," he was regarded as very intelligent and was a kind of personality in the village. In 1971, my oldest sister, her husband and their two daughters took advantage of a chance to work in a new steel plant in Suihua, a small city situated about 150 kilometers south of Harbin. My brother-in-law got a position as an agricultural machinery engineer. A branch of this enterprise manufactured and marketed a small quantity of tractors. Thanks to my brother-in-law, I was accepted the next year as a trainee in that factory.

In 1972, I left my village to join my sister's family in Suihua and started my life as an urban worker. Due to the political campaigns of the Cultural Revolution that forced many urban young people to relocate to the countryside to be re-educated, I didn't stay long in Suihua. On the 30th of June, 1974, I was sent together with 30 to 40 young workers or trainees of the steel plant to a commune called "New China" (*Xinhua*), located about 70 kilometers north of the city. The young people like me arriving from the city were grouped together. We were called "The May 1st Group."[1] I lived there for two years. During that time, we worked together with peasants but we lived in a dormitory with other young people. Since I was familiar with farm work, the peasants and leaders of the commune appreciated me very much. I was encouraged to involve myself actively in the Communist Youth League. I started then to be more interested in politics.

In 1976, a delegation from Suihua Municipality arrived in our commune to recruit young workers for its enterprises. As did many others, I applied. I wanted to go back to the city of Suihua, and of course I wanted also to be a state worker. Thanks to my hard-working attitude and my active involvement within the Youth League, I was one of those chosen by that delegation. I was appointed to work in a state-owned enterprise (SOE) in Suihua: this was the August 1st Enterprise for Tractor Parts.[2] I followed a three-year training program, mainly in mechanics. Our factory provided the same kind of social benefits that other large SOE's did: salary, medical care, living allowances, and education for the employees' children. A few years later, due to the seniority system, I even had a chance to get a small apartment of my own, enabling me to leave the small house of my sister's family. I spent 14 years of my life at this factory.

In 1978, a senior worker from our factory introduced me to Ms. Zang, who later became my wife. The worker's sister was a colleague of Zang's, and was working in the National Railway's Cement Factory. My wife's workplace was also an SOE, but richer than mine because of the prosperity of the National Railway system. She worked as a regular normal worker there. We got married at the beginning of the economic reforms. The first years of the reforms were very happy years. Like many other people, my wife and I enjoyed an improvement in our living standard. Even in this small city of Heilongjiang province, the change in our life was real. For one thing, we began to have more choice in our diet. For example, beginning in 1985, we could eat rice on a regular basis, whereas before we had eaten only corn and wheat. Besides what we got from the grain ration coupon system, food also became more available on free markets and there was more diversity. My daughter could find colorful dresses on the market as well.

At work, our performance was more linked to our production output, with the introduction of an incentive system. The more pieces we made, the more money we could earn. As the social security system remained the same as before at that time, we were rewarded with more cash if we could work extra hours. These were the years when progress and improvement of life were apparent. During those happy years, I chose to join the Party. This was such a significant event in my life that I can never forget it.

I move to Dongying City in Shandong

The end of the `80's was marked by an important change for me. Our factory's vice director, Meng, was contacted by the government of the newly built city of Dongying, four thousand kilometers away form Suihua, to set up joint ventures in order to promote the city's heavy industrial factories. Our enterprise decided to select those who would be part of this project. I had the opportunity to join in a group of more than 60 persons, all of whom were Party members and highly qualified workers, who would move to Dongying. It was not easy to decide whether to participate. I discussed this a lot with my wife, since my departure would mean that she would be alone with our young daughter, Weiwei. We took the risk because we thought it was a life-time opportunity. My salary would increase by about 20 to 30 *yuan* a month and my state worker's status would be maintained.

The development of the city of Dongying began in the early `80's, when the Ministry of Geology, along with the Ministry of Petroleum, held a national congress in Tianjin and decided to start oil exploration in Shengli by building a new terminal. Shengli oilfield became then the strategic base, with its capacity reaching 19,460,000 tons per year, and was ranked the second largest oil field of China, after Daqing. At that time it employed a total of 308,100 workers. The city was built across the Yellow River, and experienced a rapid expansion, finally achieving official city status in 1982. Today the city has a population of about 1,750,000. Due to this new economic development, it was decided to develop industry in Dongying in relation to the oilfield.

The project I took part in fell into the category of a "horizontal cooperation project," highly promoted by the government in late `80s. According to this policy, our country's technological improvement could be sped up if economies of scale could be achieved. To reach this goal, plants in the same industry located in different cities were to make an effort to combine their technologies. In fact, at that time, Dongying did not have much industrial capacity. Our counterpart was the Dongying Factory of Pressure-Measuring Instruments. As we had to bring along most of the project technology, our journey to Shandong was an impressive one, composed of tens of trucks filled with equipment and machinery. I began to work in Dongying in 1990, but my wife and daughter remained in Suihua. The administrative process to enable them to move to Shandong was quite complicated and my wife felt more secure in keeping her job in Suihua. But they were able to join me three years later.

In 1993, when the settlement of our factory was completed, a total of 120 natives from Suihua who had moved to Dongying for this project were working in the enterprise. Two buildings were also built to accommodate us and our families. Once the workers had become formal citizens of the city, my family could move to Dongying. My daughter was nine years old and went to the primary school there, while my wife was given a small administrative job at my factory.

Things at our factory went very well. We supplied mechanical parts used in extraction machineries to the near-by Shengli oilfield. The oilfield was almost our sole client and there were many factories like ours, being built around the Shengli oilfield. During this period, I was well paid, and also received an important bonus at the end of the year. I felt that the oilfield could have a very bright future, due to its production capacity and the strong support it was granted from the central government. Many surrounding private firms did quite well also. This success encouraged me to think of the possibilities of making some money by setting up my own small business. But I still felt comfortable with my position at the factory since we had accommodations provided by our factory and both my wife and I had the status of state worker.

The bankruptcy of my factory

In mid-1994, a few months after our first director, Meng, left for another job in Hebei province, things rapidly went wrong for our factory. The reason behind this turn of events had nothing to do with the factory's economic capacity: sales were increasing and new orders were still flowing in. But some people found a way to exploit our situation to make money on their own. Yu was the person who later on drove our factory into bankruptcy in 1998. As one of the people in charge of accounting for the enterprise, he had an opportunity to play with the accounting books. Yu began to issue fake invoices on which prices were artificially inflated and, of course, the system was built on a network of corrupt managers in the oilfield company. After Yu pocketed the money, he divided it between himself and the oilfield's managers. Substantial bribes were also given to some well-positioned local officials, who readily collaborated once they received their share. This embezzlement probably went on for a year, until someone who had a dispute with one of the oilfield's bureaucrats denounced Yu to the central government. Why did Beijing take this matter so seriously? Hundreds of such denunciations are probably sent every day. What we heard was that other corruption cases in Dongying were already known, but in this case the management of the oilfield has a strategic importance for Beijing. Anyway, Yu was detained in jail for about 15 days, was continuously placed under high pressure, and very likely was tortured. Under these circumstances, Yu rapidly spoke out and gave the names of his counterparts at the oilfield. According to the information Yu provided, the central government's inspectors pursued their investigation throughout the oilfield, soon arresting some corrupt directors. Due to his collaboration, Yu was released a couple days later, petrified, since he knew those bureaucrats on whom he reported were ready to murder him. He disappeared immediately and all the way up to today nobody knows where he is. The trial was quick and exemplary, with even those officials who received the smallest charges being sentenced for ten years in jail.

This turmoil in Dongying city had dramatic consequences for our factory. The newly appointed directors of the oil field refused to give us any more orders. And, since Shengli was our sole client, our factory was virtually bankrupt. Until Yu's affair, we all knew that our factory was going to stop production and shut down; it was just a matter of time.

My feeling at that time was a mixture of anger and uncertainty. I was angry about Yu and the director of our factory, who had not monitored Yu's behavior and may have had the benefit of Yu's illegal transactions. I was also angry about the oilfield company's leaders, who were intently "punishing" our factory. It wasn't fair. Why should we pay for their fault? Workers had nothing to do with this. At that time we talked a lot among ourselves. What could or should we do? Some of us thought of writing a letter or a petition to the provincial or even the central government. Others said they wanted to phone the talk show on the provincial television station. But in the end we were too cowardly or maybe not desperate enough to do anything. As a Party member, this event in my life made me doubt the Party. Of course I was not naïve; I had realized before that some people joined the Party purely for the material advantages they could have. I also disliked the attitude of some Party members of our enterprise. Still I really respected some Party members I had worked with. I was, for example, quite close to our factory's first director, Meng, who had always tried to do the best for our enterprise.

I also began to feel deeply insecure and worried about my future. My daughter was still at school; my wife would, of course, soon lose her job, too; and I couldn't find much help from my relatives. I was suddenly realizing that the system on which I had built up career was going to end. I had become a qualified worker, thanks to on-the-job training, and I had felt rewarded in being accepted as a Party member. To leave my state-owned enterprise meant the loss of all the promotion I had gotten throughout my life. Before, I had thought that my career was highly honored by my relatives and by society as a whole. I was also guaranteed full access to the health system and a pension for my old age. All these things that had made up my life all disappeared, suddenly and at once.

Because I did not have any other options, and because I felt a heavy pressure on my shoulders to find a way to earn money to support my family, I tried to forget quickly what I had lost and to begin something new. I didn't want to stay in my factory drinking tea till the official shutdown. Only the people with a low level of capabilities stayed in the factory. I really wanted my daughter, who was very good at school, to be able to have a good education. But, as you know, university fees are getting higher and higher nowadays. Today I can say that my daughter gave me the strength and courage to try something new. My wife and I spent a lot of time trying to figure out what to do. The only possibility we saw was that she would stay in the factory until the final bankruptcy, while I would apply for the status of *tingxin liuzhi* (terminate the wages, but keep the position). This status allowed me to try to set up a small business while keeping unchanged my formal affiliation with the factory. I considered, as did many of my co-workers, the status of *tingxin liuzhi* to be a more suitable or "face-saving" form of unemployment than accepting full unemployment. It allowed me to maintain the strong sense of belonging to one big family to which I had been fully devoted.

As making money had begun to be considered a measure of success, together with a colleague, I decided in 1995 to register as an individual enterprise, a *getihu*. The local government readily accorded us a license, which was not that costly. We set up a small firm close to where we live. Using our professional experience, we originally planned to sell and repair some spare parts for the oilfield. We were able to lease some machines and tools from one big company. In the beginning of the '90s, private entrepreneurship and successful private businessmen were very popular. However, I still preferred, when people asked me my profession, to say I was a state worker in my factory.

Our founding of a small business had, of course, to be kept secret from our factory management to avoid the question of a conflict of interest. Under our own name but on a smaller scale, we were performing the same activity as was our state-owned enterprise. As our clients were also identical, we were able to use the contacts we had originally acquired in the oilfield. The directors of our enterprise probably knew about our business but behaved as if they didn't know. They were probably too happy to save our salary, and to see us give some work to our ex-colleagues. Indeed, some did come over to help doing some final cleaning on products or refinishing the parts we had repaired. Even so, we rapidly realiszd that our business did not have much future. We could get orders, but they were always tiny in size and entailed time-consuming manual work. Due to the lack of investment and the unlikelihood of achieving any economy of scale, we made our living but were exhausted by the heavy workload. We tried to borrow money from banks, but we were always refused.

The search for a new job

In 1998, my factory was officially closed down. The local government proceeded with the sale of its land, buildings, and equipment in order to provide some allowance to all its laid-off workers. It took almost a year to find a firm—which turned out to be a well-known local private one—to buy the land. In 1999, each worker received 10,000 *yuan* in a one-time payment, after which we were officially laid off. It was very difficult for me just after being laid off. Even though I had known all along that this moment would eventually come, I had the feeling that part of my own personal history had ended. Even if I had initiated a private business and even if I were compensated fully, because of a lack of funding it was unlikely that such a business could develop. But that was the only way to survive.

As Dongying is still a prosperous city, things were quite well organized. The factory told us to approach the city's training centers to take part in the organized training programs that were being offered. Some of us tried to go there, but most people who did so returned quite disappointed. The feeling was that the skills being offered would not help us much to find a new job. Only some colleagues without any administrative skills or technical knowledge agreed to pursue some courses in computer training, for example. It was particularly the case for female colleagues working in the administrative field. Also everybody knew that by the time we finished the training, we would have found a job by ourselves. We also found that the training center was too far away from our home. My friends and I discussed the situation, and concluded that the best thing to do was to find a job on our own. With the money we had been given, some started to learn driving, in order to become taxi drivers. Others borrowed money from relatives and set up small restaurants. My wife had a tough time after being laid off. She tried to work in some restaurants doing miscellaneous jobs. But she was exhausted and didn't earn that much money. So she remained at home for a couple of years.

Even during these years when things were unstable and precarious, we did not envisage going back to Suihua. Officially our contractual relationship with our former enterprises there no longer existed. My wife's former employer, the National Railway's Cement Factory, was still operating, but it was far from sound. The Suihua tractor factory, according to what I have heard, was also in very bad shape and will probably close down soon. Furthermore, as you know, the situation in the Northeast was much worse even than it is here in Shandong. The number of unemployed is much higher and in Suihua, economic opportunities are rare. When I was young, my elder sister's family helped me a lot, but now it is impossible for them to do anything for us. In early '90's my sister and brother-in-law both took early retirement in order to transfer their status of state worker to their children. One of their daughters became a nurse at the hospital where my sister used to work. One of their sons, after taking part in the People's Liberation Army for three years, took the place of his father as a worker in the tractor factory. My brother-in-law died from a heart attack in 1998, the year in which his factory laid off all its workers. My nephew and his family lived on my sister's tiny retirement allowance of 800 *yuan* per month for more than three years. My nephew failed to find a suitable job and his relationship with my sister deteriorated sharply. Another reason for not going back to the Northeast was because the standard of living in Donying is higher. Furthermore, we had gotten used to the warmer weather here in Shandong. Indeed, none of my colleagues went back to Suihua.

At about the same time that our factory was shut down, I decided to stop my business working as a private entrepreneur. I had a strong feeling that I had not been able to use the past few years' time to secure a decent living for my family and me. It was a time of very hard days, and it appeared that everything I had done was useless. But then, luckily, a local friend of mine who was a taxi driver and did some small business introduced me to the Sanhe Machinery Factory, where I found work and was able to stay on for four years. The work was essentially the same as what I had always done, but, contrary to what had been the case in my previous jobs, where the factory had been just five minutes' walk away, the firm was 45 minutes from my home. This was just like being on another planet for me. The working conditions were much harder and I earned less than I had before. The work relationships with my new colleagues were also very different from what I was used to. I was not comfortable with that job and felt very tired.

For these reasons, I started to turn my attention to nearby private companies. One day, I went to a neighborhood Taiwanese joint venture which mainly manufactured metal products for export overseas. The Chinese manager, Yang, invited me to an interview. There I explained my whole story and my capabilities. He asked me a lot of questions, and I had to tell him about my childhood in the countryside, as well as my experiences in Suihua and Dongying. At the time, I didn't understand why he took an interest in the fact that I had set up an enterprise on my own. Anyway he seemed very interested and allowed me to work for a trial period in his enterprises. After a few months, as the management was happy with me, I was permitted to sign a three-year contract with the firm. With this new job, I'm at least more secure about my future. My wife now also has found a small job as a hospital janitor. We pay about 170 *yuan* a month each to the social security fund so that after our retirement, each of us can receive about 600 to 700 *yuan* a month. We also have enough money now to contract for medical insurance, for which each of us pays 600 *yuan* a year. We would like to work up to the minimum legal age for early retirement, which is 50 for my wife and 55 for myself. Our biggest pride is our daughter, who is a brilliant student in the English department of Jinan University, in the provincial capital.

Today I have lost confidence in our Party, but I do have the feeling that as a Party member, I inspired confidence. I'm sure that the fact of being a Party member has helped me to be accepted in this new company. It also helps me to get promoted. I'm now responsible for four or five workers and have less manual work to do. Very recently, the local government urged our boss to establish a Party committee at our working place. A group of seven or eight people was organized to hold a meeting once a week, and I am one of them.

Today I don't have any more interest in politics. I'm just relieved to have been able to secure my old days. I feel lucky about it, lucky to have met good people. You know, I could still be unemployed or surviving on a bad job. Lucky also to have migrated to a dynamic city with economic opportunity for a former unemployed worker like me. I'm sure that if I were still living in Suihua, things like this could not have happened. The people of the Northeast are just as good as the people of the south at doing business, but there is more opportunity here.

Antoine Kernen teaches at the faculty of Social Science at Lausanne University and at the Graduate Institute of Development Studies in Geneva. He recently published *China toward the market economy: the privatisations in Shenyang* (2004) (in French).

[1] May 1 is Worker's Day.
[2] August 1 is the anniversay of the founding of the Red Army.

The Sad Story of Zheng Erji Who Landed in the City Through the Favors Reform-Era Policies Bestowed But Rewrote the Rules While Suffering Wrongs, Once There[1]

Dorothy J. Solinger

One typically sizzling summer afternoon in the central China city of Wuhan in early September 1998, in need of custom-made sandals and disappointed that in Hong Kong no longer could a shop specializing in that trade be found, I strolled the streets, wondering if that old Hong Kong business might—like so many others—have relocated to the Mainland. About to give up hope, I noticed a small, eager Chinese woman crouching by the curb, displaying a crude signboard announcing that she was there to repair shoes. That was the beginning of my acquaintance with Zheng Erji, a woman who now calls me "*dajie*" (elder sister). I immediately questioned her: "*Ruguo ni hui xiuli xiezi, ni ye hui buhui zuo xiezi?*" (If you can repair shoes, can you also make them?). She nodded in the affirmative and soon she was at work on my first two pairs of hand-made, custom-made sandals.

I didn't give the encounter much thought at the time, just came back several days afterward and picked up my shoes. But the following year, back in the city at the same season, I decided to seek her out again. I figured she would likely still be installed in the exact same place, and sure enough she was. I was greeted as if I were a once-lost god, returned from Heaven expressly to bless her life, and that did strike me as a bit odd. It was only a few days later that I learned the significance in her life of that particular day. It happened that the very date on which I returned to her station on the sidewalk was also the day her two young boys' school bills had to be paid. Had I not arrived with cash in hand to order yet another two pairs of homemade shoes, her children would not have been able to register for that semester.

Zheng rapidly grasped the opportunity of having a foreign client who seemed interested in her situation to beg me to take her smaller son, then aged six, and, of course, without a word of English to his credit, back to America so he could be given a proper education. She explained that she was unable to afford to raise that boy properly. I was troubled by this plea, but felt utterly incapable of complying with her request. At the same time, she had also mentioned being short about 300 *yuan* per month, the very sum of money then essential to educate her children.

As I tossed in my hotel bed that night, pondering what I might be able to do to help, all at once it occurred to me that it might be possible to assist her simply by sending a monthly check in the amount of about $40 US (the equivalent then of 300 *yuan*). By the time this solution had hit me, it was still afternoon in Chicago. So I telephoned a colleague who now lives in Chicago, but who was raised in China, and asked if such a thing could be done. When he assured me it could be, I resolved there and then to adopt this family (informally, I should add). From that late summer night in 1999 until now, I have been able to claim that I have a "family" in Wuhan, and the two boys are convinced that they have a

"*Meiguo mama*" (American mother). As for Zheng Erji herself, she thereupon became my little sister, and I her *dajie.*

The basic outline of her life, which she related to me on one of our first encounters, was totally threaded through with the impacts of the political vacillations of the Chinese state after 1949. Because of the various forms of policy liberalization linked to the post-1978 economic reforms, along with her own personal mettle, soon after 1980 she was able to leave her rural, suburban home on the outskirts of Wuhan, where she had existed with a "*nongmin hukou,*" (rural household registration), eventually to work in the city at a state-owned shoe-making factory. There she met her future husband, a man endowed with an urban household registration (*feinongmin hukou*), and married in 1987. The two gave birth to a boy in 1989, who, through some awful accident (too terrible to reveal to me even after some six years of friendship), lost sight in one eye at the age of about 19 months. Mrs. Zheng keeps herself relatively well informed about government policy, and knew that if one's first child was disabled it was permitted to have a second.

But, quite unfortunately for the family, son the second appeared in early 1992, before the necessary permission for his presence on earth had been granted, according to Zheng's rendition. (Had she really even ever applied for this permission? Later details in her litany might lead one to be suspicious.) The factory in which both Mrs. Zheng and her husband had been employed precipitously discharged them both. The shock of such treatment—at a time years before the policy of "*xiagang*" (or layoffs) had been enunciated and popularized—instantly turned this man into a social outcast, impairing his sanity at the same time. According to Mrs. Zheng's account, supporting the family then became her responsibility alone; she considers her husband unable to handle a steady job. Though she has managed from time to time to find scholarship funds for her boys of one sort or another, her life became a constant struggle from that day onward.

Zheng has always adapted to her fate and dreamed of ambitions. The openness of the economy during the early phase of the state's economic reforms allowed her to move into Wuhan and subsequently to marry an urban man; it also allows her to try to earn a livelihood when her family's original source of sustenance was denied it because of other state policies (the one-child policy). But the arbitrariness of officialdom has beset her and her family time and again from the days of Mao Zedong up to the present. Yet, despite the abuse visited upon her, Zheng maintains a persisting sense of what is fair, and she continues to feel that fairness and justice is her due.

While I have kept in fairly close contact with the family, visiting it at least once a year since 1999, occasionally exchanging letters, calling long distance, and sending growing sums of money as the years have passed, I never took the trouble to sit Zheng down and hear her version of her entire story until January 2004. Once I did I found that she was truly a child of the economic reforms, at once the beneficiary and yet the victim of a wealth of shifting and haphazard policies that repeatedly threw her life awry. This discrepant finding prodded me to wonder: Is she a victim and if yes, what does victimhood connote to her? What does it prevent, but also position and enable, her to do?

As for me, I see Zheng as an emblem of a core conundrum of the economic reforms, a symbol of the paradoxes inherent in the state's relation to its own control system: While loosening old strictures released swells of erstwhile sowers into the cities, winning the privilege of urban residence proved far from the solution to all the ills of these farmers-turned-sojouners (and sometimes even –turned citizens, if decidedly second-class ones). For structural discrimination met them at the gates, as Zheng's experiences reveal all too well.

Her narrative lends several other insights and lessons, as well. One is of the mutual manipulation intertwining Zheng and the government attempting to manage her. Between the two of them, on occasion the issue of who controls (or who endeavors to control) whom, who molds (or strives to mold) whom, arises. Given Zheng's outrage and cunning, there is sometimes the scent of a draw.

Another is the theme of nostalgia for a misremembered past, a recital of justice forfeited. Whence come these values, these made-over memories? Is it the nostalgia itself that breeds the feeling of rights wronged, or instead the notion of present injustices sustained that conveys her back to a different yesteryear? And the third precept for the transcriber is the role of fabrication, of irreconcilable inconsistencies. Could it be that the mind of the recounter is so clouded by insult and grievance as to deceive itself? Zheng's presentation seems, periodically, to slip between fable and fancy as she struggles to retrieve her past.

Throughout all her travails and in rather regular brushes with state agents, there is a theme that crops up in Zheng's autobiographical account with some regularity: she insists on fighting for what she wants, even if she knows her plans counter the law or current regulations. Mostly, she takes it upon herself to live by her own lights, to the extent that circumstances--even if not the law--permit. When, intermittently, she has to suffer for this, she brims with bitterness against injustice. Her constant refrain is the unfairness of officialdom and the maltreatment she has wrongly endured. I had never before pursued the puzzle of whence her conception of her own rights and deserts derived. Zheng Erji's own telling of her tale uncovered some of the root of her conviction that she deserves treatment that is righteous. I proceed to relate her life to date, as she herself would have it told.

As her autobiography commences, Zheng was born in December 1959 during the Great Leap Forward, in a rural area outside Wuhan by an hour or two. Her family had been labeled a safe "poor peasant" one in an earlier era. But, as bad luck would have it, during the "Four Cleans Movement" of the early 1960's, her father's brother was piloting a ship and earning high wages. As a result, the family as a whole was peremptorily converted to the unfortunate category of "rich peasant," certainly spelling hardship to follow. This first bit of inequity took place when the local leader instigated an investigation expressly aimed at reversing the family's label, perhaps from spite or envy.

For, Zheng avers, at that time, the family was still rather illustrious locally. For instance, Yin Zhentao, now a Vice Mayor of Wuhan, was vice director of a company under her brother's command when her brother was serving as a *lianzhang* (company commander) in the army. Later, however, this brother became a teacher and suffered attacks during the Cultural Revolution. He even became ill from being beaten, and was sent to perform physical labor. Some people, jealous of his ability, falsely charged that he had written a sentence attacking Mao. Here was the second injustice to befall her family. Zheng's lingering fondness for the past, an emotion that crops up later on in her telling, appears to have overwritten those Mao-era manufactured offenses.

In general, Zheng bemoaned, local officials disliked her parents, and the ordinary people simply followed the leaders. Perhaps this was connected to the fact that her grandfather had been in the leather business before 1949. According to her account, this man was killed by a cow cart and his business had subsequently collapsed. At any rate, Zheng attributed the family's difficulties in part to the fact that back at that time, people didn't speak honestly (*qiushi*), unlike today. The upshot was that her family became a marginalized one in the mid-1960s, as Zheng was growing up.

But despite these discriminatory slights, Zheng managed to launch herself onto a promising path at a young age, attending senior high, and even graduating (after five years of primary school, two years of junior high, and three years of high school). Of the six children in her natal family, she was the fifth in birth order but the only one to graduate from high school, which she did in 1975 (the family was unable to afford to send the others to school, all of whom had to go out to work instead). Sadly, her older sister, a very capable person, missed out on this opportunity of obtaining a higher education. Because of the manmade political "problems" in the family, this sister was also unable to find a husband.

As for Zheng herself, when Mao Zedong died, she, like many millions, whether forsaken or favored under his dominion, felt very sad. She believed "he was the state leader and had merit, had made contributions," even while she admitted that the Cultural Revolution was his "greatest mistake." Nonetheless, it appeared that her own situation was reasonably good despite the bias against her relatives. Her first stint of employment was in a production brigade (*shengchandui*), where she stayed for four years. Her pay could amount to as high as 36 *yuan* per month when she worked well. Zheng was content to see men earning more money than she and believed this to be proper, since the men worked more, and everyone was satisfied with that system, as Zheng recalls it. Overall, she reminisced, most people experienced the system as okay. People were simple then and "didn't have many opinions. If they could eat, things were all right, and everyone worked together." Could it be that this experience instilled in Zheng the notion that people who labored hard and did what was expected of them should receive appropriate treatment? But while this work was fair, she judged, and the work points people received were considered appropriate—because people discussed each other's pay together—still, Zheng came to a point at which she did not want to continue to work in the fields any longer. She found it tiring, dirty, and heavy labor, and so she decided she would prefer to work in a factory if the opportunity should arise.

Then, in 1980 or 1981, her chance arrived. The production brigade set up a shoe factory. The conditions for obtaining employment in this venture were simple: it was necessary only that a person be young and that s/he give over 500 *yuan* to the leaders. Luckily for Zheng, a new local ruling about that time held that each family could send one person to labor in that plant, and, presumably because of her more extensive educational background among the members of the Zheng family, that one turned out to be she. Somehow Zheng had amassed a personal pot of savings from her earnings in the brigade, and she was able to put out the required sum, along with some help from her family. At that time, the government had begun to encourage people to do some business and she even started to dream of becoming the factory's boss one day. But being aware that a factory could collapse (*kua*, go bankrupt) at any time, and that being a farmer was ultimately "no good" (*buxing*), Zheng resolved to master a skill so she "wouldn't go hungry in the future."

Thus Zheng began to study shoemaking. Her diligence paid off. In just three months of learning the trade, she was permitted to do some part-time work in the plant, even as she continued her efforts in the fields. Gaining this position surely also had something to do with her father's brother's personal relations. This was a man who had been a university student in the 1940s and later an engineer and vice manager in charge of inspection in Wuhan's No. One Shoe Factory. Just around that time, he had been invited back to the countryside to serve as an adviser to, and to locate raw materials for, the factory's production, once the brigade had decided to build the factory. For this man had access to sales channels, experience, and connections with places where the necessary materials could be acquired. With time, and through diligence and aptitude, Zheng did come near to achieving her goal by becoming a manager in that factory.

At this point, an armyman requested Zheng's hand in marriage. This was a person with a "suburban" household registration, which is a higher form of non-urban registration, superior to the ordinary rural registration that she herself possessed. Though she truly cared for this fellow, several obstacles intervened. For one thing, Zheng was too busy working to consider the proposition, and there was no one who could replace her at her job. But there was another, second and more weighty angle to her refusal: She considered his status—as a driver in the army—too elevated as compared with her own peasant ranking. She worried that, Should the factory close down, who would she be? Just a peasant and, married to someone of superior status, people would look down on them.

Following this wrenching choice, yet still moving along the upward-reaching trajectory she had been climbing throughout her life, Zheng came to Wuhan City in 1983. There she was set to take a position in a small-scale private factory. She had decided on her own that she wanted to study in the city, where there were more chances to get a job. Indeed, at that point she aspired to open her own factory, earn money, and develop her talents. She therefore called on an uncle—a peasant man who had been an apprentice in Wuhan in the 1940's—who was by then an employee of the city's No. One Shoe Factory, and he helped her to find a workpost. This man had been recruited into a state-owned factory in the 1950s because he had acquired a skill, such that by the 1980s he had sufficient seniority to bring his niece into the enterprise.

Once in town, Zheng lived in the home of a married sister, riding by bus to work every day. This arrangement continued for more than a year. But with time, the business in the shop was so poor that she chose to leave, moving into yet another private factory through an introduction from the first one. There she was able to reside in a dorm and to labor along with some 30 other workers. Most of her co-workers were other people from the countryside.

One of these co-workers introduced her to Qi Dongfeng, who was to become her future husband. While she did not take to him and, though during courting they often quarreled, she felt that she had to get married to satisfy society's customs. Indeed, Qi threatened to gossip about her (*shuo tade huaihua*) if she refused to marry him, so she decided she had no choice. From the start she considered their personalities incompatible, but she knew no other possible suitors, and by that time, was already nearing 28 years of age.

One seeming benefit of this union was that her marriage did enable her to transfer her employment to her husband's factory, the state-owned No. One Shoe factory of Wuhan. But because of her rural household registration, her job status was only that of "temporary worker" (*linshigong*). Still, Zheng was pleased to land such an opportunity because the factory was thriving at the time. It was her poor luck however, to fail to squeeze into the small group of people who benefited from a new preferential state policy (*youhui zhengce*) that allowed for a change in household registration status on the basis of being related—in her case married to—an urbanite.

The next year, 1989, Qi Yachuan, her first son, was born. When he was just a year and a half old, Zheng returned to the countryside to register his household status. Somehow along the way an accident occurred in which some broken glass damaged his eye, and the only hospital available was of poor quality, ill-equipped to rescue his sight. Thenceforth, he has been classified as a "handicapped person" (*canjirenyuan*), able to see in only one eye.

From that time onward, Zheng's fortune seemed to switch course and tumble downhill. She became pregnant again in 1991, just three years after her first pregnancy, in accord, she believed, with the policy that dictated that if the first child were deformed or injured in a serious way, a second birth would be allowed. But her factory discovered her pregnant condition before she had completed the proper procedures for gaining official permission for the birth. As a result, the firm's clinic refused to give her the necessary certificate stating that Yachuan was disabled. The outcome was that, at the end of December 1991, two months before second child, Qi Yaxiang, was delivered, his father was promptly fired from his job. This was a pivotal event in the saga of the family, after which abject poverty descended rapidly. The factory cut Mr. Qi Dongfeng off with nothing--no recompense, no medical care, no funds for heating in winter, no bonus. And an insurance company only provided a one-time payment of 220 *yuan* in compensation for the medical treatment necessitated by Qi Yachuan's accident.

Subsequently, Qi sold fruit to support his family, and at first was able to earn a sufficient sum because so few people had been laid off at that time. Mrs. Zheng repaired and made shoes at home and had stores sell the shoes she turned out. Business was still easy to conduct in 1992 and 1993. But soon the government forced the couple to stop their work on the grounds that they were improperly operating on the street. They were then compelled to pay 1,300 *yuan* per quarter in taxes and management fees, and were prohibited from selling if they could not pay this amount. With the rate of exactions so high, "people," Zheng admitted (presumably quite possibly including Qi and Zheng), sometimes simply withheld payment.

Around 1995, the government absolutely prevented the two of them from doing any business at all. (Could this have been because of their failure to turn over taxes? Zheng is silent on this surmise of mine.) As his wife related their history, Qi Dongfeng, hanging around in the room eavesdropping, piped in at this point that by then he had "become very exhausted and worried about his future, was under a lot of pressure, and felt he had been wronged, that the state policy on having just one child was too harsh." His former factory soon thereafter went out of business, whereupon it gave its other former workers some money, but offered none at all to Mr. Qi. And yet, for years before, he had worked very hard in the factory and had done many things to help out, he alleged, all in the hopes of getting Mrs. Zheng's household registration changed.

After selling fruit, the couple marketed vegetables and served breakfast on the street. When harassed by local officials, they would stop for a day or two or even for a couple of weeks and then resume their business. Sometimes they would change the products they sold or borrow money from relatives when straits became dire. At one point officials would not let Qi Dongfeng manage a stall of any kind. According to his account, in response to this injustice he blocked the car of an official, claiming that he had to trade to maintain the livelihood of his family. During those days, the district-level industrial-commercial bureau, public security, tax bureau, city management bureau, and the transport and environment offices united to form a general management unit, and its officers were exceedingly rude. They knocked Qi's booth over and took him to the river. Though Qi reported the incident to the "upper levels" (*shangji*) (probably the city government), everyone refused to provide any help. "They violated my human rights," he charged as we chatted. These setbacks drove Qi to feel totally unable to support his family, leading him to swallow a dose of sleeping pills, with the intent of demonstrating to the government and society that he had been wronged. The hospital saved him, however.

Mrs. Zheng persists to this day in entertaining a conviction that she would have managed to have her two children and preserve her and her husband's jobs if only she had possessed an urban *hukou*. Besides, even without the *hukou* some could have connived to persuade local bureaucrats, but Qi and Zheng were too poor to bribe officials. Anyway, Zheng reasoned, by the time of her second pregnancy Zheng was already over 30 years old, so how could she have waited to have another child until her *hukou* would be changed? Had she obeyed regulations, she would have had to wait four years before having a second baby, even had the first one been properly recognized as disabled. Once again we find Zheng Erji reformulating wrongful regulations, turning them into rules she felt were appropriate ones for her to follow.

As things stood, Zheng had difficulty proving the disability of Yachuan, the first boy. The issue here was that her husband's factory had failed to take the record of Yachuan's disability from the hospital that had treated him, and the absence of this document placed a serious roadblock in the way of the family's finding any redress. Given that first slight, the factory did not apply for the family to get permission for a second pregnancy. Mrs. Zheng presumes that the factory leaders were well aware that they had made a mistake in their handling of her situation and were therefore careful not to give the family any evidence that could be used against the firm. Here again we see Zheng rightfully reasoning that the laws or policies in question were fundamentally unfair and that, accordingly, she should be allowed to transgress them.

Another instance of Zheng's tough-minded struggles for her rights occurred when Qi Yachuan, the first boy, was in second grade, in 1996. This was the period when the government was making it impossible for the family to earn a living. Thus, combined with the rising school fees that were one product of the state's market reforms, Yachuan was unable to go to school for a time because the family lacked the funds to pay his *jiedufei* (education fees owed to attend school outside the area of one's *hukou*). For an awful period of 20 days there was no way he could enter the school.

At this juncture, Zheng "ran around everywhere" in the city, quite desperate to find help, beginning with the city's association for the disabled and even, finally, approaching those in charge of primary education at the city-level bureau of education. In her pleas, she cried out that the boy was disabled and the family too poor to finance his learning. Finally her entreaties succeeded and she managed to get the bureau leaders to present her with a certificate to be carried to the school, stating that, according to regulations, some of the fees should be reduced. Some time later, when Zheng heard of a fellowship of 200 *yuan* per year, given by a wealthy man in Hong Kong for poor students, she maneuvered to have the school recommend Qi Yachuan for the funds, because his grades were good and his family destitute. In the autumn of 2003, when Yachuan could not attend school because of mental illness, Zheng managed to get the scholarhip transferred to Qi Yaxiang, son number two.

In 1999 the government devised a new provision: that children holding a rural *hukou* whose father belonged to the category of "urban staff or worker" (*zhigong*) could switch their registration to an urban one. Zheng learned about this new policy at a meeting held by her street and resident committee leaders, a gathering held specifically to notify affected people about the change. By early 2002, Zheng had been married a sufficiently lengthy period to earn the urban *hukou* for herself as well, under the new policy. But Qi Dongfeng's status as a *zhigong* had been negated with the birth of Qi Yaxiang in 1992. Nonetheless, Zheng somehow was able to achieve the change a year later, with the assent of the street level (*jiedao*) public security, since some officials there knew about the troubles of Zheng and her children. The great benefit of this was that, henceforth, the boys were no longer required to pay the *jiedufei*, extra school fees demanded of peasant children who wished to acquire an urban education.

Moreover, once endowed with the urban *hukou*, the family became eligible for the city's "minimum livelihood guarantee" (*zuidi shenghuo biaozhang*, termed the *dibao*, for short) in 1999, a benefit directed just at urbanites. The granting of city registration also might help the parents in finding jobs one day (though it surely has not yet), and should cease the discrimination they have suffered. Perhaps most important, the family thereafter "felt at peace" (at least on this account), having developed a sense of "equilibrium in their hearts" (*xinli pingheng*). "People are people," Zheng affirmed: *"Wo shi ren, wei shenma bu gen bieren yiyang?"* (I'm a person, why shouldn't I be the same as other people?), she demanded.

A few years later, district officials forbade Zheng from repairing shoes on the sidewalk. Occasionally there were periods when the air was sufficiently clear for her to perform her work--but other times when it has not been. It is the job of the city management bureau (*chengguan*) to notify her when it is permitted to work outside and when it is not. But an unexpected blow fell in April 2003, when, in the name of "urban renewal" and "city beautification"—and for other lofty "modern" goals that go with the economic reforms—such as sanitation and cleanliness—the city summarily demolished the tiny, shoddy, jerry-built workshop Zheng had had constructed for herself, tarring it with the title of "illegal construction." And once the officials had termed the shack "illegal," there was no need to offer any compensation for its destruction. But the intractable Zheng Erji soon devised a plan to get the shack rebuilt...if only I would supply the funds. When I offered to try to get a city official to provide administrative assistance, she demurred, in these words: "As an ordinary person I can carry out this unlawful venture, but no official could get away with it."

Meanwhile, Qi Yachuan suddenly began to exhibit symptoms of mental illness, probably schizophrenia, as mentioned above. Zheng considered his poor mental health a direct result of the extreme pressure the present, reform-era high achievement-oriented, hyper-competitive educational system places upon young people. And, indeed, his illness could well have accrued from the pressures facing the family—an offshoot, in turn, of the severe labor market and the livelihood difficulties confronting the family—a fate that has befallen many in the course of China's marketization.[2] But against all odds, Zheng was nonetheless determined to find a way to get Yachuan into a better school, an objective now attained. After her persistent pleading with a district-level educational official, Yachuan's present education at a superior school is totally cost-free. In the past few years, the *dibao* that the family receives from the city government, as of the year 2004 in the amount of some 400 *yuan* per month for the family of four, has improved their lives. But the amount—which comes to under 100 *renminbi*, or just about $12.50 US, per month per person—is insufficient. Without the help she got from her appeals to me, they family would have starved to death by now, she avers.

Zheng Erji insists on breaking the law—or contravening the rules in small and not so small ways—when she determines that she must; and she almost always suffers the consequences. Headstrong and hot-tempered, she is possessed of a sense of fairness—perhaps a mix of embellished dreams of the past and the socialist slogans from the days of Mao—and she is always ready to pursue any plan she feels is right, regardless of regulations. She repeatedly persists against the odds, having a second child without formal permission, selling on the street when officials say not to, and rebuilding an illegal workplace after the first one was destroyed. And her natural grit buoys her up no matter the result, such that she is always furious when things go wrong. The economic reforms have placed her in the city, but, once positioned there, she is not content to rest in quiet, nor passively to receive the injuries and persecutions visited upon peasants settled in town. Her few triumphs over officialdom may just be a fair match for her troubles.

Dorothy J. Solinger is Professor of Political Science and Co-Director of the Center for Asian Studies at the University of California, Irvine; and Adjunct Senior Research Scholar at the Weatherhead East Asian Institute, Columbia University. Her most recent publication is *Contesting Citizenship* in *Urban China*.

---

[1]From interviews, January 11 and 12, 2004, Wuhan. All the names used in this chapter are pseudonyms, but all the people are real.

[2] "Newspapers point out, due to the competition in the labor market getting more and more intense, the pressure on laid-off and unemployed workers and a series of social problems increases the spiritual stress on urban residents and leads to an increase in their mental illness."

References:

Lehao, Kuai. "Meiyou naru dibao di 'huise qunti'" (The 'grey mass' that hasn't entered into the minimum livelihood system) *Nanfang choumo* (Southern Weekend), March 29, 2002.